Gail Hamilton

Red-letter days in Applethorpe

Gail Hamilton

Red-letter days in Applethorpe

ISBN/EAN: 9783337109516

Printed in Europe, USA, Canada, Australia, Japan

Cover: Foto ©Andreas Hilbeck / pixelio.de

More available books at **www.hansebooks.com**

IN APPLETHORPE.

BY

GAIL HAMILTON.

BOSTON:
TICKNOR AND FIELDS.
1866.

Entered according to Act of Congress, in the year 1866, by
TICKNOR AND FIELDS,
in the Clerk's Office of the District Court of the District of Massachusetts.

UNIVERSITY PRESS: WELCH, BIGELOW, & CO.,
CAMBRIDGE.

CONTENTS.

	PAGE
NEW-YEAR'S DAY: THIRTY-THREE CENTS	1
WASHINGTON'S BIRTHDAY: TREASURE-TROVE	11
FAST-DAY: MORAL COURAGE	26
MAY-DAY: BEING A BOY	43
BIRTHDAY: CATHAY'S COSSET	58
SEVENTEENTH OF JUNE: THE GOLDEN FLEECE	68
FOURTH OF JULY: MAX MARCH'S WAY OF WEEPING WITH THOSE WHO WEEP	77
THANKSGIVING-DAY: THE SPOILED DINNER	91
FOREFATHERS' DAY: THE ARGUMENT	107
CHRISTMAS: THE MAYLAND CELEBRATION	120

NEW YEAR'S DAY.

THIRTY-THREE CENTS.

ERNE was happy. She awoke in the morning with a calm satisfaction in her heart, too deep for words. She went to her little box to survey her treasures, as soon as she was out of bed, though the frost stood thick on the window-panes. There they lay, safe and sound; a bright quarter of a dollar which her uncle Meadows had given her, and eight new cents from her grandmother. There had been ten, but Erne had run up a bill for candy at aunt Rhoda's "Variety Store" in the village, to the amount of two cents, which bill, she, being an honest little girl, scrupulously paid with the first money she obtained, even though that was her holiday funds. Immediately after breakfast, she and Margaret went to make purchases. Margaret, being four years younger than Erne had only ten cents, which, with contentment, is a great deal. It was some time before New Year, but Erne could not think of waiting a single day before spending a part, at least, of her thirty-three cents. "Besides, Maggy, dear," she argued in a matronly way, "you know you are a little girl and might lose your ten cents if you kept it, so you had better spend it at once." Margaret did not particularly like being called a little girl, but she was used to it, and rather than delay the proposed expedition, she remained silent under the calumny.

The difficulty of choosing presents! If there had been only one thing that could be bought, two little brains would have been saved a great deal of perplexity; but, turned into a wilderness of toys, they looked and admired and hesitated, and could not decide upon anything.

"Meg!" said Erne, at length, unconsciously adopting a phrase that has become proverbial, "This will never do. We shall never buy anything at this rate. Now I am going into the next shop, and the first thing I set my eyes upon I shall buy."

Into the next shop they went, and the first thing she set her eyes upon was a wooden whistle, which she accordingly bought for four cents and bestowed in her pocket.

"This is for Agnes, Meg. I shall not buy anything for you, — to-day, at any rate, because you know I wish to surprise you, and you must n't suppose you are going to have anything, and so if you get anything you'll be surprised you know, — and I will not suppose you are going to get anything for me; but if you *do* get anything, you'd better buy it when I am not with you, and then I shall be surprised too."

"Yeth," lisped Meg, who was Erne's slave, by virtue of her four lacking years.

"And now I must buy something for mamma. What would you get?"

"A bittiful fur tippet," answered Meg promptly, her eyes fastened upon a little girl who had just tripped past them in such array.

"Why, Meg, child, a fur tippet would cost — I suppose — ten dollars, and I have only — let me see — twenty-nine cents. I will tell you what I have been thinking. You know Miss Landor that we saw at grandma's."

"The one with a thing on her head?" asked Meg, whose bump of language was not yet fully developed.

"Yes, a beautiful net, and mamma liked it very much, and I dare say she would like one herself, and there are splendid ones at Farley's. I have seen them through the windows, and I am going to buy one of those. Don't you think it would be lovely?"

"Yeth, I do," said Meg emphatically.

"Don't you believe mamma would like it better than anything else?"

"I *know* she would," said Meg, with increased emphasis.

They went into the shop. The nets were there, blue and crimson and black and gold, interwoven with gold beads and silver beads and glass beads in a blaze of beauty. They selected a blue one with gold trappings. "Can you tell me how much money this costs?" inquired Erne.

"Four seventy-five," answered the clerk, much louder than was necessary.

Erne dropped it as if it had stung her. Her face fell such a distance, and with such suddenness, that the clerk asked her kindly if she wished to buy one.

"I wanted to buy one for mamma," said she sadly, "but I have only twenty-nine cents. I have spent four already."

"Couldn't you buy some silk and make one?"

"Yes, I know how to net," said Erne, brightening up.

"Do you? well, here is some braid now that you could make one of."

"How much would that cost?"

"That would be beyond your means, too, I am afraid."

"Haven't you *anything* that comes in strings that would be only twenty-nine cents?"

"Well, now, here is something," said he, laughing, and pulling from a box a skein of white knitting cotton. "You can have this for four cents."

"Oh! can I? But that will do?"

"Plenty of it, I should think."

"But do people ever wear white nets?"

"We don't keep any on hand, but I should think they would be very pretty. Run a blue ribbon into them and tie it with a bow. It would be sweet pretty."

"And then I should have twenty-five cents left," meditated Erne aloud. "But I must buy a netting-needle for I have lost mine."

"Here is just the article, — ninepence, — you may have it for twelve cents."

"And I shall want the blue ribbon, too."

"And you'll have thirteen cents left to get it with, sha' n't you? Now, here is just the ticket, eight cents a yard; beautiful color, don't you think so?"

"Yes, don't you think so, Meg?"

"Yeth, bittiful," said independent Meg.

"And a yard and a half would be just about enough. Will you have it? And you'll have a cent left, to boot."

"Yes, I think I will have it," said Erne.

She parted from her quarter reluctantly, from all the cents but one reluctantly, but found consolation in the package.

"Now Meg," said she severely, as they were walking home, "be sure you don't say a word of this to any one. It must be a great secret. Mamma must know nothing of it till I put it in her hand on New Year's. You remember."

"Yeth — but — Erne."

"Well."

"What are you going to give to Martial and Rob?"

The little sly-boots had been casting up accounts in her tiny head, as to the probability of any "surprise" being forthcoming to her from the remaining cent, and was skirmishing for herself under cover of Martial and Rob.

"Not much of anything to be sure," replied Erne, remembering with consternation her diminished funds and her unbought gifts, but not thinking it wise to display any uneasiness. "Perhaps I can make them something, — but they are boys and won't care so much. And Meg, dear, I am afraid, I shall not be able to get a very splendid thing for you, but you know, — I would if I could, — and you love mamma, poor, dear mamma, it is so sad since papa went away, and you would rather she would have anything than have it yourself? — You don't want to be selfish?" This was superadded a little imperiously, because Meg hesitated. But thus admonished, Meg, as in duty bound, affirmed that she did not want to be selfish, and that she did love her mother, but she wished, at the same time, only inwardly, that Erne was going to give her something, and was, it must be confessed, grievously disappointed.

The plots and plans to finish the net in secret were many and various; but Erne understood how to use her fingers, and before the New Year came it was rounded to completion. Little cousin Peter's little fingers and little sister Meg's little fingers had often come in contact with it, and Erne steadfastly maintained that it was their touch alone which had so soiled it; but good hard soap and a dipper of hot water smuggled into her little room did good service in the way of restoring its original purity, and New Year's morning saw the net, white as snow and brilliant with blue ribbon, lying snugly in a corner of Erne's work-box. Very early the little girls were stirring. The net was to be wrapped in white paper, and laid under mamma's plate at breakfast. The whistle was to be put into Agnes' little cup, and that was all that Erne had to give. A gingerbread horse which was to have graced Margaret's plate was nipped in the bud by the untimely loss of the cent which was to buy it.

"Erne, this new whistle won't whistle," said Meg, after blowing herself purple, in vain. Erne was looking for some nice paper to wrap the net in, but she stopped to try the whistle. "It will whistle of course," she said a little sharply. "It would n't be a whistle if it did n't whistle," which self-evident proposition did not help the case, for, with all her puffing and blowing, the whistle would not whistle. It only wheezed, and that very hoarsely.

"Well," she said, philosophically. "I am sorry, but I cannot help it. Don't tell Agnes it was made to whistle and perhaps she won't know the difference. There she comes now. Put it in the drawer, quick!" and down went the whistle just as dear, lame little Agnes came in sight. She went by and down stairs, but three-year-old Peter's pattering feet pattered in. Erne's mother called her at that moment, and she ran down. Meg stood making pictures on the frosty window-pane with a pin. It was ten minutes before Erne returned, and when she came in, there stood Peter in a chair before the bureau, scissors in one hand, and the precious net in the other, all cut and slashed and ruined!

Erne sprang forward with a scream, and Meg dropped her pin with another, but it was too late, Peter looked scared and ready to cry. Erne did not scold, as many girls and many women would have done. With an unselfish self-control that could hardly be expected in a little girl, she uttered no harsh word, but only consoled the frightened little fellow with gentle words. Then with a heavy heart she sat down and wrote a little note to her mother.

"Dear Mamma: —

"I made you such a pretty net for more than a week, and spent all my money, and now the whistle does not whistle at all, and Peter cut the net all to pieces, but he did not mean to be naughty, because he did not know, and I have lost the other cent, and that is all of my thirty-three cents. O, mamma, I am so sorry, but I wish you a happy New Year all the same. Your dear litttle daughter. Erne.

"P. S. I spent all my money before I got to the others, so they have not lost anything only one cent, and that was to buy Meg a gingerbread horse, but I lost it. Your affectionate daughter,
"Erne."

Ah me! It was a very sad little face that appeared at the breakfast-table that bright New Year morning, and when mamma read the note, the little face bent low to hide the falling tears, but Uncle Meadows drew the little girl to his arms, and said cheeringly, "Never mind, my darling, you have given us something better than all the nets in the world. I saw through the open door what a brave, gentle little girl it was,— not one cross word to my little mischief-maker, and he who ruleth his own spirit is better than he who makes the prettiest net that ever was seen. Come, my pet, we will have a happy New Year yet." And Erne dried her eyes and saw light ahead.

"Uncle Meadowth," said Meg, proffering the vulgar fraction of some glass animal, "here 'th a thag that I wath going to give you. One of hith legth ith broken, and I wath n't croth about it either; wath n't I good too?"

"Ah! another accident! Did Peter break this too?"

"No, I broke it," said Meg placidly, "but you thet him down tho and he thtickth," and Meg bobbed him down on one side as never mortal stag was bobbed, and contemplated him with great satisfaction.

And there was a sleigh-ride in the afternoon, and parched corn and candy-pulling in the evening, and Uncle Meadows there all day, and so Erne was comforted for her thirty-three cents.

WASHINGTON'S BIRTHDAY.

TREASURE-TROVE.

IT was going to be a glorious morning as soon as the sun should have time to rise and declare himself. But Margaret Mayland did not know that. She only knew it was a holiday, and Uncle Arthur would be there. He made a point of spending as many holidays with them as possible since the sad morning when papa went away. Neither did Erne know what the morning had in store. She only hoped, for she was to take her first lesson in skating, and the weather was a very important matter to her. Nevertheless she gave a hearty assent to Margaret's sagacious delight "that Washington ever was born," adding by way of showing her superior prudence an additional delight that he " stayed good all his life, because you know, Meg, if he had not been a good man he might just as well not been born at all."

"No," said Meg, "we should not have had any Uncle Albert."

"Nor skating, because we should have had to go to school, like any day."

When the morning came to itself it was the most lovely morning that could be imagined. Ice enough for the whole world to skate on, and enough left to put in all its refrigerators for next summer! Icicles drooping from the roof, — ice glittering on the trees, — ice dazzling you on the wide fields of snow, — ice — ice — nothing but ice and dazzle everywhere. Yes, something else, — there running, slipping, dancing, falling, laughing, shouting, goes Martial Mayland, with his brother Robert, and his sister Erne. She cannot quite keep up with her stronger brothers, but when she calls, " Boys, don't go so fast!" Robert calls back, " We'll leave the way behind us." Martial, being the oldest, is more considerate, and says, " You let us go on, Erne, and we shall get there first, and tie our skates on, and be all ready for you." So, as Erne knows very well where to go, she is contented.

Sure enough, when she reached the pond, there were the boys curvetting, prancing, gliding, cutting rings and hearts, and doing all sorts of wonderful things, to the admiration and despair of Erne. They immediately came to her, — made her sit down on the ice, and taking each a foot, began to twist it, and pull it, and pinch it, and strap it, to Erne's no small inconvenience, though she said nothing, because they were only putting on her skates.

"Now then!" said Martial, rising, and drawing on his mittens again when they had finished, — "one, two, three, and away!"

Erne got up on her knees first, clung to the skirts of Rob's coat, then stood fairly on her feet, — not very fairly, however, for it was one, two, three, *down!*"

"O, I never can stand, — never!"

"Stand! my stars! — how do you expect to skate then!"

"But there is n't anything to stand on."

"Stand on your balance, — so! there. Just keep up straight and even, and you won't fall." Having delivered himself of this valuable piece of advice, Martial took a turn round the pond by way of variety, and Rob followed him. Erne left by herself, persevered in several unsuccessful efforts to stand, and her perseverance was at length rewarded by a successful one.

"There! Rob! — boys, look! look!" But before they had a chance to gaze at the remarkable sight, she was down again. At length, however, she gained her feet permanently, though not, it must be confessed, very confidently.

"Good!" cried Robert, — "now you have learned to stand; that is something, is n't it, Martial?"

"Yes, indeed, it is a good deal. All you have

to do now is just to strike our right and left, and go ahead."

"O, I can't move! I shall certainly fall if I stir an inch."

"No, no; if you find you are going to topple over one way, you must throw all your weight on the other. Here, we'll take you a little while, — Rob, you take one arm, and I'll take the other. Now you just slide along, — don't try to do anything. How do you like that?"

"O, it's splendid, only my ankles keep turning, and I can't keep my feet together; they keep running out and in, and all sorts of ways. O, I *shall* be down! — O, do stop!"

"No, you won't, — you can't if you keep hold of us. You must not let your ankles turn. Keep them up firm, and when you want to stop, you must not drag down that way. You never can be a good skater till you have learned to stop.

"I am sure I can stop fast enough now, — it's all I can do. What I want, is to learn *to go*." But Martial persisted in teaching her to stop.

"You must lift up your toes so, and let your heel cut in so! and that stops you. Hullo!" The last remark was addressed to a red-cheeked little fellow, who came rushing on in great haste.

"O Martial! O Bob!" he exclaimed, as soon as he was within speaking distance, — "there's been an awful great fire, and Ploffin's stores are all burnt down, and I went with father, and there were crowds of men there, and it was in the night, and the bells were ringing, and it was close by father's office! — O, it was such a great fire!"

"Not half so great as your eyes, I'll bet a cookey," said Martial.

"Mother would n't let you say that, *I* know," whispered Erne.

"Would n't let *you*, you mean," replied Martial, in a grand way, — "it's very proper you should not, because you are a girl; but it does n't signify about me."

"I don't see why a boy should talk wicked, any more than a girl."

"Bless your heart! — that is n't wicked! What is there wicked about it?"

"It is vulgar."

"Well, vulgar is n't wicked; and besides, you don't expect boys to talk like girls. Everything that is vulgar for you may not be for me."

Here Rob, who had been listening very eagerly to their little friend's account of the fire, cried out, "Martial, let's go down and see it."

"See what?"

"The fire. It's smoking now, Max says."

"Then we can't skate!"

"You can skate any time, but you don't see

such a fire as that very often, I can tell you," said Max. " Come, you can go right over that hill, — you are most half way there now."

" Do go," cried Erne, " and let me go too."

" We must ask mamma though, first. I tell you what, Erne, you can't skate, but you can run. We'll stay here and skate, while you run home and ask her; and if she says you may go, we'll let you."

Having received this gracious permission, Erne was soon gone, and soon returned with leave for them and herself if Martial would take strict care of her, and keep her by himself all the time.

" Ho, yes indeed ! " cried he, and to make sure of it, he took a piece of cord from his well-filled pocket, and with much struggling and laughing, he tied it fast round her waist and his own, so that she could only go two or three steps from him, and thus they marched on gayly to the scene of the fire.

A very black and desolate scene it was. Ruined walls, heaps of gray bricks, coils of pipes, a smouldering mass of rubbish. Crowds of men were standing around, and crowds of laborers were beginning already to work order out of disorder. They hammered on the bricks, cleaning off the mortar to use them in building again, — they dragged off and sorted the pipes to be repaired, —

boys ran hither and thither, climbing walls and jumping over obstacles, as is the manner of boys. Robert and Max joined them. Martial would have done so, but, as he said, for " having Erne in tow." So he contented himself with peering round into every nook and corner, on the outskirts, and listening to the remarks of the by-standers and laborers.

Presently Rob and Max came up, in high spirits. Max had found a pair of spectacles among the rubbish. The glasses were cracked in all directions, and the bows were blackened and bent; but he had stuck them on his little nose and marched about, looking very comical. Max said, " Lots of fellows had found lots of things, but they were all gone now." When they had seen all they wished, and heard all the stories about the fire, they started for home again. Max kept his spectacles on, and amused himself and everybody he met with his odd appearance.

" Max," said Martial, " where did you find them?"

" O, down there by that south corner. The boys said there were heaps of things there this morning early. You see Katlin's fancy store was there, and that's where they came from."

" I should think Mr. Katlin would want his things himself," said Erne. " He's lost so much by the fire, that he ought to have what is left. How came he to let you have them?"

"Why he did n't. He does n't care. You see they are not worth anything. He could not sell them. Nobody would ever buy them."

"I don't know," said Martial. "Perhaps he could not sell them to see with; but he could sell the bows for old silver."

"O, but they are not silver. I asked the boys; they said he did not keep anything but German silver."

"That alters the case."

"Now you don't know," interposed Robert. "Perhaps he had one pair real silver ones, and perhaps that is the pair you found. I should n't wonder a bit."

"I should wonder a good large bit," said Martial. "However, we can settle that matter in no time. Hand them here, Max."

Max gave them. Martial took something out of his pocket, I believe it was some kind of chalk, and rubbed it on the sleeve of his coat, and then rubbed the bows on that. The three children crowded around him.

"It is n't silver, is it?" said Max, rather excited. Martial did not reply. "I know it is not silver," he continued, as Martial stopped to examine the effect of his polishing.

"So do I," said Martial, abstractedly.

"There, I knew it was n't, Rob."

"But — it — is — gold! Hurra!" cried Martial, swinging them around his head. "Max, your fortune is made."

"No, it is n't gold though, is it?" said Max incredulously.

"It is n't anything else. Why, just look, — see how it shines!"

"You're a lucky fellow, Max," said Robert. "Make your father buy them, and you'll get ever so much money."

"Yes," said Max; but he looked as if he did not think of what he was saying. Then he stopped suddenly, and said, with a very determined air, "I sha'n't keep them."

"No, I would n't," said Erne, softly.

"Yes, I would," exclaimed Robert, loudly.

"What will you do with them?" asked Martial.

"I shall carry them back and give them to Mr. Katlin. You see, if they are worth anything he ought to have them. I think they are just as much his as if they were in his shop."

"But you don't know that they were in his shop," said Robert. "Perhaps they never belonged to him at all; and if you don't know, I should think you had as good a right to them as anybody."

"O, nonsense!" exclaimed Martial; "don't befog yourself in that way, Robert. You know they were Mr. Katlin's, as well as you want to know anything. There was no other store in the building where they could have been. Of course they were his. But I say he ought to have gone and picked up his things, if he wanted them; and if he does n't, why, he must expect other people will."

"I suppose he had n't time," answered Max; "or perhaps he had so much to think of he forgot it."

"Or perhaps he did n't think anything had stood the fire," said Erne.

"Any way," continued Max, "I shall carry them back. Wait for me, I sha'n't be gone a minute."

A minute passed, and two, three, five minutes, and Max did not come, — nor did he appear till they were almost home.

"Well," cried Robert, "what did he say?"

"Gave you a dollar, I hope, as a reward for your honesty," said Martial. Max was breathless from running, and only shook his head.

"What! did n't he give you anything?" said Martial with pretended astonishment, "after such remarkable self-denial."

"I did n't give them to him," said Max.

"Whew! Got sick of your bargain?"

"No, I could n't find him. I went all round. Nobody knew where he was."

"So you brought them back again?"

"No I did n't. I went and put them just where I found them."

"Well, I *de*-clare," said Martial, stepping backward and putting both hands in his pockets, "if you are n't a greater fool than I took you for!"

"I don't care," muttered Max, simply because he did not know what else to say. He looked and felt ashamed, as if he had done something silly, though he could not tell what.

"For pity's sake," continued Martial, "what good did you suppose that would do? Are n't there fifty boys round all the time to pick up everything?"

"There was n't a single boy near when I put them back, and I don't believe anybody saw me."

"But they'll be there again after dinner, and some scoundrel, likely as not, will get them, and that's the last of it. Much good you have done by your honesty."

Max looked as if he would like to cry; in fact, Erne thought he did shed a tear or two as he turned away to go home, and she felt sorry for him, and said to Martial, "I don't think you need to have scolded him so."

"Scold! I did n't scold him. It is none of my business. But I do hate to see a man make a goose of himself."

"I don't think Max is more of a goose than you." Erne had been made bold by the sight of the little boy's grieved face.

"Just you look here, little upstart!" said Martial, good-naturedly, "don't you undertake to teach your elders. You mind your dolls, will you? That's your look-out. I'll take care of myself and Max too."

"I move that we ask Uncle Arthur about it," said Rob, who had been very quietly turning the matter over in his head.

"I second the motion," replied Martial; "not that I have any doubt as to my own opinion, but to satisfy you."

When they reached home, they went at once to Uncle Arthur's room and knocked. He bade them come in.

"Are you busy?" said Martial.

"Tolerably; but if your business is very important, as it generally is, I suppose mine can wait, as it generally does."

"Well, Uncle Arthur, it is moved and seconded that Max March is a downright simpleton."

"O no! it is not," burst out Erne; "that was n't it at all. We said — "

"Now you just stop and let me have my say first. One at a time,—sha'n't she, Uncle?" So he began at the beginning, giving a very correct account, with a few amendments by his brother and sister, and closed with,—"Now, in my opinion he's the biggest goose out."

"And we don't think he is," said Rob.

"And you want my opinion as to the correctness of your views?"

"Yes, sir."

"Very well, if you will give an exact definition of what you mean by 'goose,' Mr. Martial, it will help me very materially in my decision."

"Well, sir," said Martial, coloring, "I don't mean precisely that he has feathers and web-feet, but he has acted in a very silly way, and he might just as well have kept the glasses, as to carry them back to be picked up by the first boy that comes along."

"Now we're going to have a lecture," said Erne. "I always know, when Uncle Arthur runs his hand through his hair so, he is going to say something."

Her uncle smiled, took Erne's round chin in his hand, and said, "Yes, I am going to give you a lecture, because I want you to understand the difference between one thing and another. You are partly right and partly wrong. Max did not make the best possible disposal of his goods"—

"There!" said Martial, snapping Rob's ear.

"Because it would have been better to have given or sent them to the owner. As it is, he will not be likely to hear of them again. In all other respects Max has acted nobly."—

"There!" said Rob in his turn, trying to snap Martial's ear, but not quite succeeding.

"And the good he has done, the right he has done, is so much greater than the folly, as not to make it worth taking into account in deciding upon the action. The latter was a mere error in judgment. The former was a firm stand against temptation. He has not much money, and I have no doubt struggled hard, though only for a moment, against the desire to keep the gold. His purpose was to keep himself pure from the sin. He did it, when he returned the spectacles to the place whence he took them. So far from calling him 'a goose,' I call him a truthful, honest, noble boy. He was wise in a wisdom which is of God, a higher and truer than any worldly wisdom. He was true to the great principles of right and wrong, though unskilled to tell what was best in a mere money point of view."

"But, Uncle Arthur, do you think it would have been stealing if he had kept the spectacles, seeing he found them?"

"I wont say, my dear, that every one who did

take anything stole it; but I say that if Max had kept them, it would have been wrong for him. He felt that they were not his, but Mr. Katlin's, and he would have wronged his conscience by keeping them; and I am sorry that you said anything which may lead him to regret doing a right thing."

"There!" repeated Rob again, — "you see I was right."

"You aggravating little villain!" exclaimed Martial, with mock fury, — "I wont be insulted by a baby! You had no business to be right when your older brother was wrong!" and seizing his coat collar, and dexterously applying his foot, he laid Robert at full length on the carpet.

"And you, — what business had you to be wrong, when your younger brother was right?" said his uncle, laying him by a similar movement "along-side" of Rob; and so the lecture ended in a very un-lectural frolic. But the truth sunk none the less deep into their hearts for that.

FAST-DAY.

MORAL COURAGE.

GREAT, round, and fiery, the April sun was going slowly down, and through the swelling buds of the Baldwin apple-tree his yellow light glistened on the face of two little girls, perched on the top of the orchard gate. They loved the sunshine, and lived joyously in it all day long, yet now they wished and waited for it to sink behind the gold-rimmed cloud; for it was "Fast-day," and Matty's mother always observed it as strictly as the Sabbath, and not till sundown were the eager feet and hands released from a sometimes tiresome restraint. On this particular day, Matty's most intimate and dearest friend, the receiver of all her twelve-year-old secrets, her bosom companion in doll-dressing, and vulgar fractions, and candy, Chatty, had come to stay all night with her, and it seemed to the children as if sunset would never come.

"No, never, I do believe," said Matty, kicking the heels of her Sunday boots impatiently against the gate.

"Nothing ever does happen when we want it," added Chatty. "Now, if we were playing, and had to stop at sundown, that big, old, saucy face would go galloping into the sea just as fast as he could, but because we want to be rid of you, you just tease and mock us, you ugly old fellow, indeed you do," and shook her fist laughingly at him, but he hurried none the more.

"Then they sat still awhile. Chatty broke the silence first.

"Matty," said she, "don't you think Fast-day is rather funny?"

"Funny!" echoed Matty, "no indeed! I don't see anything funny about it."

"But somehow it seems to be half and half, neither one thing nor another. You go to church, yet it is n't Sunday, and you have a fine time, and yet it is n't a week-day."

"I don't have any finer time than I do Sunday, nor so fine, for I don't go to Sunday-school, and I don't like it so well as I do Sunday.

"O, I do, better; all the boys come home and it's right fun. And we have a grand dinner. Why, it's next to Thanksgiving."

"We don't have any dinner, only a little bread and butter."

"I wonder what Fast-day is for, any way. What is Fast-day? It's no faster than any other day."

"No, that isn't what it means. To fast, you know, is not to eat anything. Breakfast is when you break your fast. You don't eat in the night, so you fast, and in the morning you break it."

"Then *we* don't have any Fast-day at all, because we keep eating."

"No, I should think not," said Matty musingly.

"But it isn't a real Fast-day to anybody," continued Chatty, "because everybody eats something. If you don't have a nice dinner, meat nor pudding nor anything, then it's a fast pudding, but it isn't a fast day."

"Some people don't eat any dinner at all."

"Then it's a fast-noon, but it can't be a Fast-day unless you don't eat anything all day."

"Well, *I* don't know."

"But what is it for?"

"Why, we always have one you know every year, and go to meeting, and all that."

"I know *that*, but what is it all about?"

"Fasting and prayer," mused Matty, "that is what the paper says, you know. I suppose it is because we are wicked and we must pray to be forgiven; O, and isn't that the time when we are thankful for the crops, and the weather, and health, and all that?"

"Ho!" laughed Chatty. "No, that is Thanksgiving. Fast always comes in the spring. We don't have any crops in the spring."

"O yes, I remember now. But I dare say that is why we have it, because we want to get the good crops. In the spring we pray to have them, and in the fall we pray because we 've got them. That must be it."

"But then we can pray just as well and eat dinner too," she continued, after a short pause.

"I don't know about that," said Matty, "the Bible says we must fast."

"Where does it say so?"

"I don't know where, but it does."

"I never saw it, I don't believe it says a word about it."

"O yes, it does. My mother says so. Anyway, my mother keeps fast, and so I shall, just as she does."

"So shall I, just as my mother does, but I should like to know all about it, and I mean to ask my mother, because if —"

"Gone!" cried Matty, leaping down from the gate with a mighty clapping of hands, for a great slice of the sun had disappeared.

"No. Going, going, but not gone," said the more patient Chatty.

"I don't care. Sundown does not mean the whole of the sun," reasoned Matty. "Come, he 'll be out of sight by the time we get up stairs."

They went into the house and took off their bonnets, and, my little friends, if any of you want to know what "Fast-day means," and "what it's for," and "how to keep it," and "all about it," I advise you to do as Chatty concluded to do, "ask your mother."

Just as they were going up stairs, Matty's father called to her. "Matty, I want you to go to the store and buy me some tobacco." He was an excellent man, hard-working, poor, self-denying in many things, but I am sorry to be obliged to say, he *would* use tobacco. Matty looked disappointed a moment, as she thought of the dolls waiting for her up stairs, but her father said he would build a fire, and get the room warm, while she was gone, and Chatty was very willing to go, so they started merrily. It was only a little way, and the errand was soon done. But the tobacco had not been wrapped very scientifically, and it rubbed against her shawl, and troubled her.

"I mean to take the paper all off," said Matty.

"No, indeed, you will have to hold the nasty stuff in your hand, then," exclaimed Chatty, with childish inconsiderateness.

"I guess if it is clean enough for my father to put in his mouth, it is clean enough for me to hold in my hand," said Matty, a little nettled.

Chatty saw that she had made a blunder, but

she was not wise enough to know what to say to redeem it, so she said nothing.

Groups of half-grown boys were beginning to gather in front of the shoemaker's shops, and at the corners of the streets. They were ill-bred and rude, and often jeered at the two little girls.

"Hullo! tobacker's fell," cried one.

"Look here! Give a fellow a cut, can't you?" asked another.

"I say, now, what's your hurry? I want to fill my pipe."

Chatty was a little alarmed. She was not used to such things. "O, do let's hurry," she whispered.

"Dear me; they won't touch us. I'm not afraid," replied Matty.

"But do put the tobacco under your shawl, so that they won't see it."

"I won't do any such thing. My father sent me to get some tobacco, and I guess I'm not ashamed to do what my father told me to. If they're a mind to laugh, I don't care. I'm not afraid of being laughed at." And she held the tobacco out at half arm's length, very stiff and prominent. Of course, every boy they met had something or other to say about it, and when they reached home, Chatty was ready to cry with anger and fright.

"Chatty is such a coward, you can't think, mother," said Matty.

"There were ever so many boys, and they acted so," said Chatty, deprecatingly.

"But *I* was n't afraid," continued Matty, rather pompously. "I just held it right out — so, before them all, and did n't care a bit. Chatty wanted me to put it under my shawl, but I would n't."

"And a very foolish little girl you were, too," said her mother.

"Ma'am!"

"And conceited and selfish, withal."

"Why, mother!" Matty's face had grown wondrous long.

"What could induce you to make such a simpleton of yourself?"

"Why, mother, did n't my Sunday-school book tell all about moral courage, and the boy that was n't afraid of being laughed at?"

"Yes, my dear, but that was entirely different. He was doing what he ought to do, and was not to be laughed into doing wrong."

"Well, I am sure, so was I doing what I ought to do. Father wanted me to go for the tobacco."

"He did n't want you to hold it in front of you, like a walking advertisement."

"But, mother, do you want me to be afraid of being laughed at?"

"I want you to be so afraid of it, as not to do anything to provoke it. There is no merit in persecution or ridicule. If we suffer for Christ's sake, very well, but if we draw reproach upon ourselves just for the sake of showing that we don't mind it, it is both foolish and vain. Chatty showed a great deal more sense than you. You ought to have held the tobacco out of sight. There was no good to be gained by exposing it, and an evil to be avoided by not exposing it. You ought, also, to have had more regard to Chatty's feelings, and, since there was no principle at stake, to have saved her annoyance. But everything had to bend to your vainglorious feeling, 'I am courageous, I am not afraid.' So you see your moral courage has turned into folly, self-conceit, and selfishness, as I told you before."

"Well, I declare!" said Matty, quite crestfallen at this new view of the case, yet self-convicted of its truth.

"For my part," said Matty's brother, Robert, who had come in during the latter part of the conversation, "I think people make a great deal of fuss about moral courage as if it was some great thing. *I* think it's the easiest kind of courage."

"Do you?" said his mother quietly.

"Yes, ma'am; for instance now, if I was going along in a wood, and had a great deal of money in a dark night, and a robber should come along with a pistol, and I had n't any, and should threaten to kill me if I did n't give him my money, I should be afraid; but if he should want to make me rob people too, and should just threaten to laugh at me if I did n't, do you think I should mind him? No indeed. He might laugh a year right straight off and I should n't care."

Their mother was called away at that moment and their conversation was turned to dolls and dresses.

The summer came and went, and their father's strong frame was bowed with illness. For weeks he lay on the verge of the grave, but Mrs. Ashley's prayers were answered, and he went out once more into the sunshine of the happy day. Yet for a long time after he was pronounced out of danger he was weak and unable to take that active part in supporting his family which he had been accustomed to do. Consequently a heavier burden fell on the wife and mother, but she bore it, nobly and cheerfully. Many little wonted luxuries were silently given up, that poverty might not press on her children's hearts, and they, though they knew few of her sacrifices, rewarded her mother's heart by their prompt obedience and tender love. Matty particularly learned to be careful and saving, thoughtful of the happiness of others, self-denying and patient. The summer had brought no fairer fruit on the earth than had sprung up in that young heart.

"See what has come for you," said Matty to Robert one fine morning in November, as he came in from the frosty air with his cheeks all aglow.

"What is it? where did you get it?"

"Mrs. Harcourt sent it. It's going to be a jacket for you."

"It's a horrid thing!" and Robert looked down contemptuously on the cloth which Matty was holding up to show.

"I am sure it's a very pretty color," said she, deprecatingly.

"It's a horrid color."

"Why, it's just the color of the covers of mamma's Tennyson, that Uncle Blake gave her, that you liked so much."

"So you liked the color of the shell that he gave me, but you wouldn't want your hair to be of that shade. No more do I want to be dressed up in mamma's Tennyson. I tell you I can't wear it, and I won't!" and Robert looked very wronged, and fierce, and determined.

"O, don't say so, don't!" pleaded poor Matty; "when you know how poor papa is sick, and has to keep working all the time, and it's as much as mamma can do to keep us whole at all."

"I don't care, I'm not going to be dressed up like a dancing doll. I won't wear it, so, there!" and he turned away, but he spoke in a choking voice, and his bright eyes were full of tears.

Robert was very kind and affectionate, and loved his parents. He knew that they worked hard, and were often troubled and careworn. He knew that when Mrs. Harcourt gave the piece of blue cloth to his mother, it answered a question which she had been anxiously asking for many days, "How shall I spare money enough to buy Rob a jacket?" Still, it was so different from the other boys' jackets, and he thought it would look so funny. I dare say no one would have noticed it, but he thought every one would, so it was all the same to him. Besides it would have done no harm if it had been noticed.

Mamma entered just then. She saw the cloud on the face of her beloved ones, and inquired the cause. Neither spoke immediately. Tender-hearted little Matty did not wish to grieve her mother or Robert, and she did not see how she could offer an explanation without doing both. As for Robert, he would have found it rather difficult to speak, if he had tried. But mamma saw the cloth in Matty's hand, and she divined the trouble.

"What is it?" she said cheerily; "does n't Rob like his new jacket?"

"O mamma!" sobbed he, coming forward, "I am dreadfully sorry, but I can't wear it. I shall look such an object, and all the boys will laugh."

It was out, and Matty stood gazing at her mother, the perfect picture of distress.

"Why, you dear little simpletons," said mamma, "why have you been working yourselves up into such a tempest? One would think the fate of the world depended upon a jacket."

Matty had evidently expected her mother would go into hysterics, or that something terrible would happen, and she was greatly relieved by the very calm way in which she took it.

"Then, mother, you don't care at all?" said Rob, starting up from the lounge where he had thrown himself.

"Yes, O yes, I care at all, — but I don't want you both to look as if there never was going to be any more sunshine in the world."

"Won't you just tell us how you do feel?" said Matty.

"Yes, tell us exactly what you think about it," added Robert.

"Very well, I will try to give you my views on the subject. Let us look at the cloth. It is a very pretty color. It is very good, stout, warm cloth. Still, I know it is different from other jack cts, and will very likely attract attention. I should be very glad if my Robert was brave enough, however, to wear it, for all that. I should like to know that he was strong enough to do what he thought right, even if his schoolmates should laugh at him. But I shall not insist upon his wearing it. I shall let him do as he chooses."

"But, mamma," said Robert, sadly, "you will think all the time that I am an ungrateful and selfish boy; and that will be about as bad as wearing the jacket, and I sha'n't have any peace of my life, any way."

"No, indeed," said his mamma, smiling, "I shall think no such thing. I shall be a little disappointed in finding you less strong than I supposed, but you are a little boy still, and I cannot expect you to be as immovable as a man. When you are older, I expect you will be as firm as the solid rock in doing right,—and even now I know you would be willing to do and to suffer almost anything for your parents,—except being laughed at."

This comforted Robert not a little. "But what will he do for a jacket?" asked Matty. Her mother's face lost its smile.

"I don't wan't any," said Robert quickly, "I will make the old one do."

"No, my dear, the old one is almost worn out

now. You cannot make it last through the winter." There was a pause. "I can think of one thing — but —"

"What is it?" cried they both, seeing their mother hesitated.

"I do not know that I ought to mention it, as it will involve a sacrifice on Matty's part, that I am not sure she ought to be called on to make."

"O never mind me, mamma," cried Matty, eagerly. "I shall not care in the least. I will do anything."

"You remember the cloth Aunt Matty gave you several weeks ago for a cloak?"

"Yes, ma'am," said Matty, flushing up to the roots of her hair. "You mean, mamma," she added, bravely, after a moment's silence, "it would make a good jacket for Robert."

"Yes, my dear."

"No, I won't do that," said Robert stoutly. "I won't take Matty's cloak. I would rather freeze stiff in a snow-bank."

"Matty can have a cloak of the blue cloth."

"I should think the brown was enough for a cloak and jacket, too," said Matty.

"O no, Matty. These round cloaks take more cloth than you suppose."

"Then he may have it; I don't care."

"But I tell you I won't," persisted Robert.

"Do you think I am such a thief and a robber? Why should you look like a fright any more than I?"

"I shall not look like a fright, shall I, mamma?" Matty had had a struggle, at first, to give up the cloak which she had anticipated so long, — but now the struggle was over, and she heartily wished Robert to take it, — particularly since she was afraid he would not.

"No," said their mother. "The cloak will be less singular than the jacket; in fact, I think it will look very well. And as Matty is quite willing you should have it, and as it will be very inconvenient for your papa and me to buy you another jacket, I think, Robert, you would better take it. You need not fear making Matty unhappy, as I am sure she would derive more pleasure from seeing it on your shoulders than on her own."

"Yes, that I should," cried Matty, "especially when I know that he would feel so miserable in the blue cloth."

So it was decided that Robert should have the brown, and Matty the blue cloth.

But Robert was not so happy as Matty thought he would be. He was not satisfied with himself. He remembered that his mother had said she was disappointed in him, and he felt that he had not been brave and manly, — not even so brave as his sister, whom he had often laughed at for being afraid of a mouse, or a spider. The more Robert thought of it, the more dissatisfied he felt, and one morning he stopped in the midst of his dressing, stamped his foot on the floor, and exclaimed, "Now, Robert Astley, stop this. You have been a coward, you know you have, and a mean coward, too. You have palmed off on your sister, what you were ashamed to wear yourself. Right about face!"

The moment he was dressed, he went straight down stairs to his mother. "It's no use, mother," he began. "I had rather be hung outright, than pricked to death with a needle. I won't be haunted all winter by the ghost of Matty's cloak. I'd rather wear a jacket with all the colors of the rainbow than feel mean."

"Too late!" said his mother, smiling, and holding up the blue cloth, which was already cut into cloak shape. Matty smiled too, but Robert was in consternation.

"You need n't care in the least," said Matty. "It's a very pretty cloak, and I would a great deal rather see you wear a jacket like the other boys."

"And as you have finally got the victory," continued his mother, "you may as well get all the comfort you can out of the jacket. You will know better what to do the next time."

"That I will, indeed, but I wish I could do something, or wear something now, that should make all the boys kill themselves with laughing at me, so you should see I am not afraid of them."

"I think it is hardly worth while to prove you by bringing about a wholesale slaughter; but do you remember, my dear, a little talk we began to have last Fast-day about moral courage, and how easy you thought it would be to be laughed at?"

"O yes, mother, I remember it perfectly, but then I meant doing something *wrong* rather than be laughed at. Here, you know, it was n't anything wrong that I was afraid would be laughed at, but —"

"But a color."

"Well, now, yes I give up, *for that time*, but you'll see I will have no end of moral courage after this. I'm not afraid of anything, see if I am. Come on, Matty, let's fight," and he doubled his fists at her in most valiant wise.

MAY-DAY.

BEING A BOY.

MRS. MAYLAND was spending two or three months away from home for the sake of having her little Agnes under the care of a physician; Uncle Albert had put Martial at school. Rob and Erne were invited to make a visit at their Uncle Meadows's where was a houseful of cousins, and little Meg was left under the care of Mrs. Deecomb, who was a cousin of Mrs. Mayland's. Meg often visited there and was much delighted with the arrangement. Augusta Deecomb had an older brother named Nathan, who was very fond of little Margaret, and her cousin Joshua, about her own age, lived at the head of the lane about twenty rods off. When Nathan was at work on the farm, Joshua was very glad to play with Augusta, and they were excellent friends. I believe they never quarrelled, but agreed exactly on all points. When Meg first went to them they paid her royal honors; but after the novelty had worn off they became rather lordly themselves, and vied with each other in browbeating, ordering, and otherwise snubbing Miss Meg, who was always with them, and who was only too glad to be browbeaten, ordered, and snubbed, if she might thereby purchase the privilege of accompanying them in all their excursions. When they took the trucklecart and rambled into the woods, she trotted behind. When they lay in ambush for stray squirrels, she squatted beside them, and both kept digging their elbows into her patient sides, and whispering, "Kee' still! kee' still!" making themselves, with their poking and their whispering, twenty times as much noise as she who scarcely breathed in her anxiety to keep still. When they came home from school they always appeared around the turn of the lane in one line of march, Joshua and Augusta ahead and abreast with their tin-pails, and Meg trudging along a step or two in the rear like a little puppy.

Happy as they were together, I am obliged to confess that Joshua was in some respects a coward. Although he truly enjoyed the company of his girl friends, yet no sooner was Nathan through with his work, and ready for play, than Joshua left the girls, flew to him, and even began to take on airs, look down upon girls, and make himself in many ways pompous. At such times Augusta betook herself to Meg, and found solace in concentrating her authority and dignity upon her, and tyrannized over her with unparalleled and absolute rigor. Now I suppose you think Margaret must have been a very miserable young person; not a bit. Snubbing is nothing when you once get used to it. Meg, besides being quite used to it, did not even know that she was snubbed, and was as happy as a queen.

Augusta's favorite amusement, during her short divorces from Joshua, was to play at being boy. She enacted Joshua, and Meg, to her supreme delight, was dubbed Nathan. If she ever showed any symptom of rebellion against Augusta, it only needed to say, "There! no boy, no boy!" and Margaret crouched at her feet again. They used to go up garret and trick themselves out in Nathan's old jackets, caps, and waistcoats, and made themselves up into true scarecrows you may well believe.

Ambition grows by what it feeds on, as you will learn when you grow up, if you do not know it now, and Augusta, from being willing to give all she had in the world, if she could only be a boy, came at length to conclude that she would be as much like a boy as possible, and made herself quite disagreeable sometimes by persisting in following the boys wherever they went with her faithful attendant Meg.

So when Nathan announced one May-day morning that he and Joshua should turn the holiday to account by going a-fishing, Miss Augusta, like Peter of old, announced that she also should go with him.

"You!" ejaculated Nathan, scornfully, "you would make a pretty figure trampoosing through bogs, and woods, and brooks, and brush, a dozen miles."

"Poh!" said Augusta, tossing back his scorn, you need n't talk. I can trampoose as well as Joshua."

"You can lag, and bother, and make an outcry at a spider. That's what you can do. See here," he said to Joshua, who just then entered, armed and equipped, "Gusty here wants to go a-fishing. I've a great mind to let her, just to get rid of her."

"That won't be getting rid of her," replied Joshua.

"Yes it will. She'll soon be tired of beating round after us, and stay at home, and give us some rest."

"Well, I'd let her then," said magnanimous Joshua.

"See here now, Gusty, you've got to keep up and not cry, and do everything. If you will be a boy, *be* a boy. Which will you carry, the luncheon or the bait?"

"The bait-box is the smallest. Let Meg take that. I'll have the luncheon."

"Meg? Meg too?" queried Nathan, doubtfully. "Well, yes, we'll finish the girls this time. Come along." I do not think that Nathan was over-courteous, but boys are very apt not to be over-courteous to their sisters.

If Mrs. Deccomb had been at home, I suspect there might have been some objection to little Meg's starting on such a tramp; but Hannah had been left in charge for a day or two, and she never could refuse the children anything, and believed, indeed, that nothing was so likely to injure them as being crossed. So she contented herself with giving them strict injunctions on no account to lose sight of Meg, and they all departed together. Through green woods, by many a narrow path, and often with no path at all, tramping along the sweet May morning, what a glorious thing it was to be a boy, and how Gusty plumed herself, and patronized Meg, and scolded her when she did not keep up; but suddenly a terrific shriek burst from those little lips, and there stood Meg, with the bait-box at her feet, and both arms wildly tossing.

"What's the matter?" cried Nathan.

"Ugh! eh! ah!" gasped poor Madge.

"It's a snake bit her," suggested Joshua.

"It's a fit," trembled Gusty. "Jane Smith's baby has 'em."

"O," moaned Meg, recovering her breath. "Baits is worms! I ony peeked in!"

"*Horrendum visu!*" cried Nathan, in mock alarm. "What did you think 'baits' is, — elephants? So much for having girls round." And he scooped up the long, wriggling, disgusting worms, and strode off, Meg following, very much cast down. But no wonder a little girl was scared when she peeped into an innocent-looking little box, and found she was carrying in her own hand so loathsome a company; for, talk as you will about everything being the work of one Creator, I believe that the same hand that made worms made them loathsome to people in general.

"O! there's the brook," cried Gusty, as the bright water leaped suddenly into view. "Is that where the fishes live?"

"Yes; but further down. We must ford this." And Nathan began to take off his shoes and stockings, and roll his trousers up away above his knees. So did Joshua. So did Gusty to a limited extent, for though she could dispose of her pantalets, her dress became a serious consideration. Meg began also to exhibit her light fantastic toes in high glee.

"Stop that," suddenly ordered Nathan. "You are not knee high to a trout. I'm going to back you. Put on your stockings and shoes."

"O, I want to go in the water," moaned Meg.

"And be carried away by the current, and lodged in the old mill-wheel?"

"No," sighed Meg; and hurried on her shoes again. Gusty meanwhile followed Joshua down to the brookside, and stepped daintily and on tiptoe into the water. It was rather cold, though the day was warm. The mud squeezed in between her toes and tickled her. She lifted her feet up with "a suck," and then they sank deeper in. Then she came to the pebbles and they were not pleasant, and some large stones rolled over when she stepped on them, and came very near letting her into the water; but she kept laughing and shouting, "O, it's splendid!" and then the water grew deeper, and wrapped itself around her knees, and she had much ado to keep her clothes dry, and at the same time hold on by her luncheon basket, and her shoes and stockings. But still she kept shouting, "O, splendid! splendid! Don't you wish you were here, Meg?" While Meg, on Nathan's shoulders, was frightened into pale silence, expecting every minute to go down, splash! into the water and be drowned, and could only cling and cling, and wished in her heart she were safe home again.

"Hold up your dress," cried Joshua to Gusty; "you are getting it all drabbled behind." Gusty gave a quick clutch at it and dropped her shoe.

3   D

The brook, nothing loath, bore it merrily away. In great dismay she called to Nathan, who was quite across, and he rushed along the bank, plunged in and brought it safely ashore, but somewhat soaked. A little prick in her foot disturbed Gusty, and looking, lo! a little black, slimy thing was sticking fast on it. She kicked with nervous fury, but only wrenched her knee. The black thing gathered and broadened himself, but did not come off, and after three seconds of frantic effort, she screamed nearly as loud as Meg had done, "O, get it off! get it off!"

"It's nothing but a bloodsucker!" said Joshua coolly, snatching it up. "Afraid of a bloodsucker!"

"I'm not afraid of a bloodsucker," declared Gusty; "but he bit me."

"Why did n't you get him off then?"

"I did; but the harder I shook, the harder he stuck. How are you going to dry your feet? Did you bring a towel?"

"A towel! O my! a towel a-fishing! No; roll 'em and dry 'em so, on the grass." Gusty did as well as she could, but gravel and grass and straws got on rather faster than the wet got off, and when Nathan came up with the heavy, wet shoe on the end of a long branch, she snatched it, shook the water out, stuck her foot in, and walked on, the water dropping from her dress down upon her stockings, and soaking from her shoes up.

A tossing, tumbling, chattering, saucy, helter-skelter, head-foremost little brook it was, — never still, never tired. Meg's little feet began to feel as if they would be tired one of these days, but her Spartan soul gave no sound. "Why don't you catch some fishes here?" she asked, with a sidewise view to resting.

"No fishes to catch," answered Nathan. "Got to go along to where it is stiller. Fish can't live in a cataract." And the little feet plodded patiently on.

"Ship ahoy!" roared Nathan suddenly to Gusty, who was furtively inserting her fingers into the luncheon-basket.

"I don't care. I am as hungry as a bear," answered Gusty coolly; and a large slice of bread and butter began to appear and disappear at one and the same moment.

"So be I," echoed Meg. "Let's have dinner now."

"Dinner now, — before we've begun. That's always the way with girls." But notice: deep into the basket went Nathan's fingers, and quick down his throat went quite as large a slice of bread and butter as Gusty's, and they all lay around on the grass, chatting and resting.

"Let's not fish," suggested Meg. "Let's call it a picnic, and have a good time."

"Yes, we shall fish," exclaimed Gusty severely. "It's just the day for it. A picnic is nothing. Did you bring a hook and line for me, Nat?"

"Yes; but we sha'n't catch any fish. It isn't a good day. Too bright. Fish wont come out when the sun burns 'em."

"Ought to have a cloudy day," said Joshua, anxious to display his small stock of piscatorial wisdom.

"There's clouds now," said Gusty, blinking up into the sky.

"A mackerel sky, — that's nothing."

"What's a mackerel sky?" queried Meg.

"A sky to catch mackerel under," answered Nathan.

"A sky that looks like a mackerel's scales," said Joshua. "A spotted sky."

"Derived from the Latin, *macula*, a spot," continued Nathan, learnedly. Meg began to look bewildered.

"I should n't like to catch a whale," she broke in at right angles, as usual.

"You won't be likely. Don't be afraid," said Nathan, soothingly. "This brook isn't large enough. You can't find whales short of Mill's pond."

"But simple Simon found 'em in his mother's

pail," persisted Meg, who had implicit faith in Mother Goose.

"O, what a guy girls are!" shouted Nathan.

"But she's such a little girl," interposed Gusty, agonized for the reputation of her sex.

"Ho! a boy no bigger 'n a walnut would know better than that. Come, come along, all of you. Here, take the lines. Now you look out when we get to a place. And don't you talk. You keep still. Bimeby the fish 'll come, — trout and roach and all of 'em, perhaps."

"O, how shall I know? I want to know what I catch," asked Gusty, eagerly.

"You 'll know fast enough when you catch 'em, I guess. There's roach, they're shy. They'll come up and smell, and smell, and bite the back of the hook. Trout are all red and blue and mottled; there'll be lots of them. There's a place where the stream runs along under the bank, and it's all black, and the old fellow likes that. He backbites furiously. You look out now. He's a game fish. And there's suckers, — kind of long and narrow and lazy. O, well, you catch most any kind. A polliwog's better than nothing."

And so they tramped on and on and on, — dropping their lines into the water now and then, but pulling them out when Nathan gave the word of command, and rambling further down the stream,

— through thickets and underbrush, across rich, loamy fields, over moist meadow-lands, now ankle-deep in muck and moss, then scrambling as well as possible among thorns and briers, leaping from green slimy rocks to green slimy bogs. Ah! what a tramp!

"You 've teared your dress a little," panted Meg in a breathing-hole.

"You 've teared yours about off; hush up!" retorted Gusty.

Both hats had fallen off, and hung on their necks, and, with very hot cheeks, and very red faces, they pressed on. Nathan had caught three suckers, and that was the amount of the whole party's success. Occasionally Meg would scream, "O, I 've catched a trout; I know I have!" But her trouts and her suckers generally turned into an old branch, or a mass of dead matted weeds. Then she began to be so wholly tired that she forgot her vassalage, and grew cross, and it was, "O, I 've got a rock in my shoe!" and all came to a halt till the forlorn little shoe was righted. "O, my line is snapped by a tree!" And Nathan took it in charge. Finally, in sheer despair, out came the whole truth, exploding in a violent "crying-spell," as poor little Margaret shrieked, in a very rage of fatigue, "O, I want to go home! I 'm so hot, and it burns me and sticks to me! I want to go home!"

Now Meg was generally so plastic and passive, that, when she did set up for herself, everybody knew that something must be done about it. So nobody scolded her, but the two boys gave up their "traps" to Gusty, and made a "lady's chair" to carry Meg a little way and rest her. But Gusty was almost as tired as Meg, and with their fishing-poles, a basket, and a box, she was fast finding life a burden. More than once she stumbled over the fishing-rods, and once she scratched her arm with a hook. Presently they reached a place where the fence came quite down to the water's edge, and indeed half-way across the brook. The bank was rocky and uneven. The boys got safely over with Meg, and Nathan told Gusty to stand stock still till he came back to take the rods. But nothing was farther from Gusty's intention than to stand still. She tilted her rods against the fence, stepped cautiously along the rock, and to the top of the fence. The fence was rather crazy. Her weight made it sway and stagger, and the rods slid down against her. Not knowing what was going to happen, she gave a spring, forgetting that she might just as well tumble in as jump in. She did indeed land on the rock as she intended, but with such force, that she bounced from it head foremost into the brook.

Joshua stared, Nathan laughed, and Meg screamed, "O, she is drownded!" But she was not at all "drownded,"—could not drown if she had tried. She scrambled up thoroughly wet, and scrambled out thoroughly disgusted.

"It was all you! You did it," she cried furiously to Nathan.

"How'd I do it, for pity's sake?" gasped Nathan, rolling on the grass in a most exasperating fit of laughter.

"Because you — because — because you made me lug all the things."

"Well, the things did n't get you in, did they? You just plumped in yourself. O you frog! Come here, and let's wring you out. O dear! who but a girl would ever think of jumping head first into a trout-brook?"

But Gusty was not to be wrung out. She was too thoroughly drenched for that, and there was nothing for it but to turn about and march home, which they did;—Joshua, to his credit be it said, sympathizing with Gusty too much to laugh at her, but too cowardly to stand up for her like a man, and therefore somewhat silent; Nathan, joking and laughing very provokingly, but swinging Meg, now on his back, now in his arms, and now coaxing her to trot along by his side; and Gusty either silent or savage. The worst of it was, that for days after, two little faces were the most dreadful little faces you ever saw,— sunburnt, red, swollen, and sore, so that one could hardly recog-

nize them. Continued application of cold cream restored them after a while to their natural shape and color; but for a long time Gusty's face had a way of turning marvellously red whenever Nathan chose — and that was mischievously often — to ask her how she liked being a boy.

On the whole I am rather sorry I have told you this story, and I think I will not do so any more, lest you begin to think girls ought not to roam about with boys; but I want girls to go trouting and rambling and frolicking in the fields and woods just as much as boys; only, if they have not been used to it, they ought to be a little careful how they attempt hard tramps in the beginning, especially if their brothers do not give them a very hearty invitation! Gusty made her experiment under disadvantages. She tried too much for the first time, and Nathan was not so sympathizing as might have been desired; but after all, I don't know that it did her the least harm. It is better to be sunburnt than shadow-paled, so I advise all you little girls to tie your hats close upon your heads, put on your rubber or stout leather boots, and strike straight out into the woods, where I doubt not you will have such fine frolics, that the first you know your brothers will be stealing out after you, and begging you to let them come too!

BIRTHDAY.

CATHAY'S COSSET.

"WELL, of all the March winds that ever I see, this beats all! If that door has blowed open once, it's blowed open twenty times this morning!" and Hannah wiped the soapsuds from her soaped and wrinkled hands preparatory to going into the passage to shut the refractory door. "I'll have a new latch on; I won't be bothered in this way. It's all along of that —— lawful heart, child! what are you standing here for like a post?"

It was a very pinched and blue and cold little face that looked up wistfully at Hannah, turning her so suddenly from her soliloquy; but the blue lips gave no sound. Now Hannah, a stout, brisk, rough kind of a woman, with arms as brown as a berry and as big as a (small) stove-pipe, had a heart just as large and very soft. The child's sad eyes looked straight into that heart of hers, so, instead of telling her to go away, she said, "Well, come in and get warm, at any rate. You want that if you don't want anything else. How on earth anybody can manage to get so cold, I can't conceive." The last part was muttered rather than spoken; and in her warm kitchen, over her wash-tub, it *was* difficult for Hannah to form conceptions of cold.

"If you please, ma'am, I should like —— " began the child tremulously, and hesitated.

"Out with it," bounced Hannah, "a piece of bread and butter, I suppose."

"O no, ma'am, no indeed; I am not a beggar; I only wanted to know, is Mrs. Deccomb at home, and could I see her?"

"Why, yes, she's at home, and I suppose you can see her, but — I dont see what *you* can want of her," she would have said, but did not, only added, "Well, come along, I'll show you where to go; there, third door."

The little girl gave a faint rap, and a pleasant voice said, "Come in." She entered. Mrs. Deccomb sat by the fire sewing. She looked up rather surprised at the strange form, and for a moment the child was too much frightened to speak; but she presently faltered out, "If you please, ma'am, I wanted to ask you, — do you know, — anybody, — would like to have me work for you?"

"Work for me?" said Mrs. Deccomb, smiling,

as she glanced at the slight figure, trembling now from cold and excitement. "Come and warm yourself, and we will talk about it." The little girl sat down on a cricket before the bright wood fire, and its glow seemed to enter into her heart, for not only did her blue cheeks turn red, but a new light danced in her sorrowful eyes.

"What is your name, my dear?" said Mrs. Deccomb kindly.

"Cathay Horn, ma'am, and I'm not a beggar.

"No indeed, but you wish to work and get money for yourself, is that it? Have you no father nor mother?"

"O yes, ma'am, but father has been sick; or, he has n't been very sick, but the cow has, and the cow died, and father was n't very well, not well enough to work and get another."

"Yes, I think I have heard of you. You have moved lately to the mills, have n't you?"

"Yes, ma'am; but father was took sick, and he could not work. It's his hand that is sick, and he can't work no more 'n if he was sick all over. A — a — *forger*, or something dreadful, grew on his hand."

"A felon, — was it?"

"Yes, ma'am, that was it, and when the cow died he felt very bad, and we all eat so much, it takes so much — " Cathay hesitated.

"How many brothers and sisters have you?"

"Well,—a good many; I don't know exactly how many, but I can tell you their names."

"Very well, let me hear them."

"Yes, ma'am. There's Molly, and Wad, and Joe, and Life, and Dud, Patty, Becker, and Judy, and the baby, and Hetty besides, O and me!"

Mrs. Deccomb could hardly help laughing at the rapidity with which she spun off the names. "And do you all live at home?"

"No, ma'am; Molly minds Mrs. Rice's baby, and Life — his name is Eliphalet, but we call him Life for short — he is learning a trade at Mr. Parsons's, and Joe and Dud are in the mill. The rest of us live at home; — and last month I had a lamb that Mr. Rice gave me, — an early lamb to take care of, — and he's so lovely, and his name is Pearl. I named him, and he knows me, and has a ribbon round his neck, and O, I love him so; and we eat so much that father can't hardly get enough for us to eat; and, he does n't say I must n't keep the lamb, but Patty says it's a shame, and how I ought to sell him and buy money with him, — but O, I can't sell him, and I thought last night I would see if I could n't work for somebody and buy money that way, and then I could save my lamb till he's grown up into a sheep, and then he'd have little sheep, and I'd have a flock, and sell 'em and get a great deal of money." Cathay had risen in her eagerness, and stood before Mrs. Deccomb with flashing eyes.

"My dear child," said Mrs. Deccomb, gravely, "which do you love best, your father and mother, or your lamb?"

Cathay stood silent a moment, and then said slowly, "I love my father and mother best *up*, and I love my Pearl best *down*. Pearl is my baby."

"And you would rather keep Pearl, even if it does hurt your father's lame hand to work for him and the rest of you?"

"But Pearl does n't eat much; not much more than the baby, and besides, I want to work, and feed him myself."

"Yes, but suppose you should sell Pearl, and give your father the money, and then work besides, and instead of feeding Pearl, feed the baby. Don't you see it would help your father, and his poor lame hand could rest?"

A few moments' silence and Cathay said firmly, "I cannot sell Pearl. He loves me. He sleeps with his head in my lap. I am his mother, and he is my baby. I can't let the butcher-knife go into him and make him bleed. I'd just as lief it would stick into me, every bit."

"A kind and faithful little girl," said Mrs. Deccomb. "I 'm glad you *are* so true; but now see:

I will give you five dollars for Pearl, and he shall not be killed, but he shall come and live with me, and have plenty to eat, and Nathan and Augusta shall take care of him. You may give the money to your sick father, and I will look about and see if I can find a place where you can work. Now do you think you can give up the company of your pet, — you see that is all, he will be just as well treated, — can you do it for the sake of helping your father and making him feel that his little Cathay loves him?"

It was a great struggle for Cathay, very great; but her grave lips presently said, "Yes, ma'am."

"Very well. By and by I will send for the lamb. And as you are such a brave and true little girl, I think I shall be able to find a place for you where you can help your father."

Mrs. Deccomb's gentle words were a great comfort to Cathay, as she walked home; but when Pearl met her and rubbed his head fondly against her hand and jumped and frisked for joy, her heart failed her. She dropped on the grass, threw her arms around him and cried. But Pearl did not seem to mind her tears. He was as happy as ever. "O Pearl, darling, darling little Pearl, you 've got to go. But I love you just the same. It is n't because I don't love you, never think that of your Cathay. It 's because you eat so much.

You don't eat too much either, darling. I like to have you eat, I'm sure; but it's because poor father's poor hand is sick and I can buy money with you. Now, Pearl, darling, will you remember me, my baby? Don't forget Cathay, who loves you, and will think of you all the time, and will say her prayers for you every night. I don't give you up because I don't love you, darling, but for my father to see that Cathay loves him; and I am his Pearl, and he must not see me crying, must he, Pearl? So don't cry, dear. O darling, I wish we were in heaven."

But Cathay dried her eyes, and told her father that Pearl was going to live with Mrs. Deccomb; and when Mr. Deccomb's man came, she only gave Pearl one final hug, and then walked quietly over to the farm, and saw him happy with the children there, and then she gave the five dollars to her father, and his kisses and pleasure comforted her; but when she went to bed at night, she plunged her face into the pillow, and softly cried herself to sleep. Poor little Cathay!

The March winds murmured themselves into April breezes, and the gentle rain pattered down on the seeds that lay sleeping in the brown earth's bosom, and they awoke and peeped into the light. The sun, too, met them graciously and wooed them out, and the grass grew green on the hillsides, and April melted into May, and Cathay's birthday came. Cathay was very happy, for Mrs. Deccomb had invited her to a little party, and "certainly I shall see Pearl," she thought.

"Yes, you shall see Pearl," said Mrs. Deccomb, when Cathay asked her. "We will all go out into the fields by and by, to get some flowers, and then you shall see him. You can play a little while first."

Cathay thought she would much rather see Pearl first, but she was too polite to say so, and she began to play with Erne and Meg Mayland and Gusty Deccomb and Max March and the others, and became so much interested that she quite forgot Pearl, till Mrs. Deccomb told them to get their bonnets, for they were going after the May-flowers.

"Cathay," said Meg, "I know something."

"No you don't know anything. Hush!" said Erne, pinching her.

"Yes, I do, about Cathay's lamb," persisted Meg in a loud whisper.

"Yes, I know," said Cathay, "I am going to see my Pearl, — your Pearl, — that is, — but O it *is* my Pearl that I used to have."

"Yes, he's right over there," said Gusty; "but we must get the May-flowers now, because we're not coming home this way, and then you know perhaps we'll make a wreath for him, for we love him almost as much as you do."

"No," said Cathay, shaking her head, "that can't be."

"Perhaps Cathay does n't want anything on his neck," said Erne.

"No; I'd rather have his very own neck and my arms round it than anything else in the world."

"Remember Erne," said Gusty significantly, "Cathay does not want anything on his neck, *not anything.*"

So they rambled on, swooping up blue and white innocence by the handful, and purple violets by ones and twos, hunting through the woods for the trailing arbutus, guided by the sweet scent which it could not hide, and filling their souls with the warm spring sunshine. Presently Max said he had left something at a turn of the road, and he must go back; "but Cathay," he added earnestly, "there certainly is some May-flowers under these leaves. You see if you can't find them before I get back, and don't you stop hunting till I get back, and *don't you turn round!*"

"No," said Cathay, too eager for the flowers to feel curious about what he meant.

In about five minutes little Meg uttered a great shout, and Cathay started up, and there, leaping and bounding towards her, as fast as his four slender legs would let him, came Pearl, pure and white and happy, just as she had left him six weeks before, only a little fatter and fairer; and Cathay dropped on the ground in her old way, and he jumped into her open arms, and rubbed his nose against her face, and Cathay hugged him and squeezed him in all manner of unreasonable ways, as the most patient of lambs was never squeezed before. But suddenly she stopped; for round his neck was a blue ribbon, and to the ribbon was fastened a card, and on the card was written,— what do you think?—

> "Dear mistress Cathay, will you have
> A birthday gift of me,
> And let a little lamb once more
> Your darling baby be?
> For surely all such generous
> And noble-hearted girls
> Deserve to be presented with
> The very best of Pearls."

Do you think Cathay said no?

And as Mrs. Deccomb took Cathay into her own house to help Hannah, of course Pearl could eat as much as he pleased without robbing any one.

SEVENTEENTH OF JUNE.

THE GOLDEN FLEECE.

THEODORE and Theodora, twins, found themselves at home in Applethorpe, on the seventeenth of June, one of the finest of summer days, while all the older members of the family, and indeed a large portion of the grown-up people of Applethorpe, had gone to a neighboring city to witness the laying of the cornerstone of a monument, which was to be erected in memory of heroes who had fallen in defence of their country. Theodore and Theodora would have been very glad to go, but as they could not they contented themselves with depreciating the occasion. "I am sure it will be far finer at home," said Theodora, when the carriage rolled away. "We should have to hear a speech and behave properly, and we have only lost the drive."

"Yes," answered Theodore, who could not quite forget how charming the horses looked.

"Besides," added Theodora, "I don't care so much about the seventeenth of June any way. It was just fighting and fighting."

"Yes," said Theodore, doubtfully; "but they fought for their country."

"I know it; but everything was just alike. One man fought with another man. If now there had been anything dark and dreadful, dragons, monsters, and such things, there would be some pleasure in it. Do you know I think we live in a very stupid age. Everybody that we read about used to find wonderful things, and do wonderful deeds, and we just don't do anything to signify."

"Indeed we do!" cried Theodore, his patriotism roused. Steamboats and cars and the telegraph and sewing-machines and our clock that has the shoemakers and blacksmiths on it. I don't believe the little Noahs were ever waked up by such a clock."

O, to be sure we have plenty of those tiresome things that nobody wonders at in the least. But I mean something really wonderful and splendid, like Aladdin's lamp you know, — discovering things, — caves full of gold and rubies, — and rocs and such things, — and swords that stick in the rocks like King Arthur's, till the right man pulls them out and he is the true king, and gets his throne back again, and everybody else is killed in battle, — O, and enchanters and dwarfs that turn into beautiful princes and marry beautiful princesses, — and the Golden Fleece, and all that. Of course I don't mean Noah and such people."

"I don't suppose there ever were really any such people," said Theodore, thoughtfully, pulling up the grass around him.

"Indeed there were, and I think,—I really think there are such things now, and I think I know where to find them."

"Where?" asked Theodore, amazed.

"Will you go and search for them with me?"

"I don't believe there is any such thing."

"Maybe there is n't, but I think there is, and at any rate, would it not be grand to try? Only think, while they are all making speeches and crowding around a monument that is n't built, we shall be ADVENTURERS going over the ocean like Sir Walter Raleigh and Ponce de Leon and that Jason man after the Golden Fleece!" and Theodora tossed back her brown curls, and flashed enthusiasm from her blue eyes into Theodore's quieter soul. "Let 's go," said he.

So they ran down the avenue and off into a side-path that led into the woods, till they came to a beautiful little brook that bubbled and foamed and rippled and rolled and murmured and sang cheerily, merrily, in and out, now black under the shade of trees that bent low to its plashing waves, now sparkling in the June sunshine, now purling among violets, now dashing against rocks, and altogether the wildest, quaintest little brook you ever saw, till it fell softly and sweetly into the arms of a broad pond, or lake, that lay snugly tucked in among the wooded hills.

"Now," said Theodora, solemnly, "if we follow the brook down to the lake and then go over the other side, there is a place where you have to go between two big trees, and under some more. I have often seen it, — and it looks dark there, and I am persuaded if we go in, we shall find a stone or something that leads to a cave, and if we say 'Open sesame,' or something, it will fly open, and we shall go in and see all manner of beautiful things, and the Golden Fleece, and any way fairies, I have n't a doubt."

"But how are we to get there?" said practical Theodore, who had a way of seeing lions that escaped Theodora's eyes. "We can walk and wade in the brook, but the pond"——

"Walk and wade! People don't walk and wade in search of adventures. We must bring the boat, of course, and this is the Mississippi River, and that is the Atlantic Ocean; and we are in search of the fountain that has power to quench disease and bring immortal youth." (Theodora was recalling her history lesson.)

The boat, which was a little one made on purpose for them, was brought out from its nook under a willow-tree. Theodore took an oar, and they started on a voyage of exploration; suddenly Theodora bethought herself that they had no sail.

"Never mind," said Theodore. "It's a row-boat. It does n't matter. We never have sails to it."

"We never went after the Golden Fleece before," said his sister, with quiet majesty; "and it is n't a row-boat, make believe. It's a great ship, —
> Its sails are all swelling,
> Its streamers float gay'

and how can its sails swell if it has n't any sails?" So she jumped out, brought a long stick, tied her white apron to it, held it up at the prow, and they started again. It was not very smooth sailing. They kept hitting against rocks, and running aground with a force that often sent them both headlong; but they only jumped up again, leaped into the water, pushed the boat off, and went on just as gayly as before. To be sure they became thoroughly wet and draggled, but they were used to it, and it did not hurt them in the least.

With red faces, and brown arms, and melancholy-looking clothes, they had almost reached the pond, when they suddenly heard the barking of a dog. Theodore stopped rowing and listened. "It's our old Silver, and there she is; I wonder how she came here."

"I don't know, I'm sure, but she must go

back the same way, for we can't stop to see to her."

"But something must be the matter with her. Just see how she looks and barks, and keeps running back and forth."

"Perhaps somebody is hurt in there. That's the way dogs do in books, you know. Let's go and see."

"But we can't get our boat ashore over that log."

"We can take off our stockings and shoes and wade. You know we shall not be in search of a Golden Fleece, only after a dog."

Their dignity being thus provided for, they were soon ashore, and followed Silver into the wood. She ran before them with every manifestation of delight, and stopped before a fallen hollow tree-trunk, looked up into their faces, wagged her tail, and did everything a dog could do to express her opinions and wishes. A kind of purring, whining noise seemed to come from inside the trunk, but a large log had in some way rolled down before the opening.

"I do believe there is something inside this trunk," said Theodore.

"A woodchuck," suggested Theodora.

"A snake, perhaps."

"Or a deer."

"We don't have deer; but let's see if we can't get the log away and find out."

It was pretty heavy, and had fallen with so much force as to bury itself in the loose earth, but their united efforts at length removed it, and lo! two poor little half-blind and quite bewildered, disconsolate-looking puppies!

Poor Silver's joy and gratitude knew no bounds. She fondled them with all her might, stopping occasionally to caress Theodore and lick his hand, her whole heart overflowing with dumb dog love and gratitude.

"What shall we do with them?" asked Theodore. "We must n't leave them here."

"No, something might happen to them again. We'd better take them home and feed them, and they'll be ours, and we'll call them Theddy and Tid. Yours shall be Tid and mine Theddy."

"Then when I say Tid, you won't know whether I am speaking to you or a dog."

"Well, Tid Silver, then I shall know. Now let's carry them home."

Theodore took them in his arms and tried to carry them; but they kept slipping, and he kept stumbling, and neither was very comfortable. So Theodora said she would put on her apron again, and carry them in that. Then Theodore transferred them to her, old Silver looking on meanwhile with great satisfaction. She seemed to know that the children meant *her* children nothing but good.

It was harder going up the brook than it had been coming down; but stout hearts make stout arms, and they had fastened their boat in its proper place, and landed their passengers, when Theodore suddenly exclaimed, " O, Tid ! " and stopped short.

" Well ? " asked Theodora, quietly.

" Where 's our golden fleece ? "

" We have n't any. Only two little silver dogs. That 's all."

" But we were in pursuit of adventures ! "

" And have n't we found them, I should like to know ? " answered Theodora, a little pettishly, for she never liked to acknowledge that her ends were not gained, and accordingly generally made her facts suit her theory. " Is n't it an adventure to rescue poor dumb brute animals from death by starvation and pain, when they would die if it was n't for you, and their mother bark her throat out, and die of a broken heart, and be a poor miserable orphan mother all the rest of her days, I should like to know ? "

Theodore was deeply impressed by this burst of eloquence, and silently gave in his adhesion to her plans.

So their Golden Fleece turned into a pair of half-starved puppies, which are not quite so grand as the heroes of the seventeenth of June; still I think a kind act is worth all the Golden Fleeces that ever were or were not in the world."

FOURTH OF JULY.

MAX MARCH'S WAY OF WEEPING WITH THOSE WHO WEEP.

IN the village of Applethorpe was a little, old, low, brown wooden school-house. In this little, old school-house, one bright June day, a score of rosy, healthy, happy children were making the old roof ring with shouts of laughter. It was "noontime," that is, the hour between twelve and one, which, in this school, was the time for eating dinner and playing. Most of the children came from a distance, and brought their dinner in little tin pails. As soon as school was out at twelve, there was, for a few moments, a great commotion among these tin pails, and then they were ready for play. At this particular time they were running wild, over, or in, the game of "Shun it." You do not know what that is? I will tell you. In the first place you set up a stick of wood, or anything that will stand on one end; then, any number of children join hands in a circle around it, and pull "every which way and t' other," as one of my young friends described it to me,—

everybody's object being to make somebody else knock the stick down, and not to knock it down himself. "A rather rude kind of play?" I beg your pardon, it is not rude at all. Rough, I grant you, but not rude. "You'd like to know what I call rude, then?" Why, I thought you were rude when you called Loo a "telltale," the other day; and Fred was rude when he saw a woman's veil go flying off in the wind, and did not run after it, but only stood and laughed. But a good, wholesome game, that makes the cheeks glow, and the eyes sparkle, and the hair fly, and the voice ring, and that does *not* excite any wicked feelings, is very far from being rude.

One of the happy group of which I am speaking was Quinny Ford. She was the smallest there, — a slight, delicate little figure. Her schoolmates tried to urge her not to play, for fear she should be hurt; but she was brave and gay, and high-spirited, and she wanted to do what she saw other people do. When they found she was determined to play, Max March took her under his especial charge. He was large, and strong, and gentle, and very fond of Quinny. So she kept hold of his hand very firmly, and though she was twisted and pulled about in all directions, she kept her feet, till, at one violent jerk, the little boy who held her other hand let it go, and poor Quinny was hurled to the floor. Her leg struck against one of the benches, and the pain was very great; but she was afraid to cry, because she thought they would blame her for playing. The blood rushed up to her hair, and down into her neck, — but she shut her lips close, and did not cry. The children stood around her, and Max bathed her leg in cold water. She begged them not to tell the teacher, and presently hopped to her seat. When she recited, she only had to stand up in her place, which she managed to do on one foot. But alas! when school was done, and she tried to leave the room, she could not put her foot to the floor. Then she was so frightened that she could command herself no longer, but burst into loud sobs and cries.

"What *is* the matter, Quinny?" said her teacher, alarmed.

"O, — I — can't — walk!" sobbed Quinny, — and then the children told the teacher the whole story. She tried to comfort the little girl, and asked Max if he would go to her father's, and have him come with his wagon to take Quinny home.

"O, I 'm afraid to stay here alone," cried Quinny.

"Well, dear, Lucy Dixon will stay with you till your father comes. I would stay myself, but I must take the cars to-night, and I am afraid I shall be late."

"Please ma'am," said Max, "if you will send one of the other boys for Mr. Ford, I'll stay with Quinny. Jem Hale lives close by."

So the teacher despatched Jem Hale, and sent the other children home, that Quinny might be more quiet, and left her and Max by themselves. He sat on the floor, rubbing her leg very tenderly. She had always been a little afraid of him before, but she forgot it now, in her great pain, and greater terror.

"O, Max," said she, tearfully, "do you think I have broken my leg?"

"No, indeed; because if you had — there, does that hurt you?"

"No."

"Well, if you had broken it, that would have hurt you terribly, — so you would scream right out."

"Do you think I shall ever walk again?" The tone was so mournful, that Max, boy as he was, felt the tears come into his own eyes, — into the back part of them, you know!

"Why, yes, little Quinny; I think you'll walk just as well as ever, in a few days. If you don't, I'll make a truckle-cart, and I'll be your little pony, and you shall drive me wherever you want to go, — would n't you like that?"

Quinny smiled through her tears, but said, "I'd

rather walk"; — and presently added, as sadly as ever, "And I sha'n't be able to go to Fourth of July!" Another burst of tears from her very heart. "O, I wish I hadn't played! O, I wish I had done what you told me! I shall have to stay at home Fourth of July, all alone!"

"Now, don't cry so, Quinny, — don't! Perhaps you'll be well by that time, — and if you don't go I'll stay with you, and you shall be my May Queen, and we'll have a picnic, and Charlotte shall come ——"

"No," said Quinny, more calmly, — "I sha'n't let you lose the party for me. You are very good to stay with me now, but you must n't stay then. I shall try to be good. I shall have to stay at home anyway, and there will be no good in crying about it."

Presently, Mr. Ford came and took Quinny home. The doctor was called, and he said the cords of the limb were injured, and gave her mother some liniment, and said she must be kept very still. She did not feel ill, — so it was very hard for her to lie still; but worse than that was it to think that the Fourth of July was fast coming, and she could not go to the picnic. Her little schoolmates came in from time to time, and they were very full of their plans, and expressed very loudly their sorrow that Quinny could not go.

Only Max, — he said nothing about it, — he had an idea in his head.

The first day of July, after he had been telling Quinny about matters and things at school, he bade her good morning, and went down stairs, and through the kitchen into the pantry, where was Mrs. Ford. He stood awhile in the door-way. She was working over butter, and did not see him. Pat, pat, pat, went her fat hands on the fat butter, and sputter, sputter, sputter, came the buttermilk into Max's face; but he did not mind it, — only made wry faces.

"Good morning, Mrs. Ford!" said he presently.

"Bless me! — Max, is that you? Good morning! — I did not see you. How you scared me!" Pat, pat, pat, all the while.

"Did I?" a short pause, — "Mrs. Ford —"

"Well, child?"

"I don't suppose Quinny could go to Fourth of July, could she?"

"Poor child, no; I'm afraid she can't. I'm sorry, for her heart was set on it." Another pause.

"She sits up all the time now, does n't she?"

"Yes, but she has to keep her leg still. She is not to use it, or move it, any more than if she were lying in bed."

"But could n't she be carried there in a wagon,

and go very slowly, and be quite still while she was there? — just lie and see the others?"

"Well, dear, perhaps she might; but our wagon is broken, and, you see, I am afraid some harm would happen to her there. I can't go myself, for I don't like to leave Gran'ther; and she might get excited, and something might happen. I should worry about her the whole time." A still longer pause. Max was gathering courage. Out it came, at last, —

"Mrs. Ford, I hope you won't think me teasing, but I have a truckle-cart, — I had it made on purpose, — I made part of it myself. It is very easy. You can put pillows in it, and make it just as soft as a bed. If I would promise to take *very particular* care of her myself, all the time, would n't you let her go?"

"Well, I declare, Max March, if you a'n't a real kind boy! Well, I declare, I don't know as it would hurt her. She does want to go so much. You 're real careful, I know, and ——"

"O, I 'll be *so* careful!" interrupted Max, eagerly.

"But, bless me! you can't drag her all the way. You 're only a little boy, for all. Your body a'n't half so large as your heart."

"Well, three of the boys are going to help me. I asked them. They said they would if you would let her go. Nat Deccomb and Rob Mayland, and ——"

"I declare,— I don't know. If she keeps on, and it's pleasant Tuesday, I guess she can go. But don't you say anything to her about it; for if, after all, she could n't go, she'd be worse off than before."

Max wanted very much to tell her "right away"; but he promised not to lisp a syllable of it, and in order not to forget himself, he resolved to stay away the rest of the day, and as the next day was Sunday, of course he would not be there. So there would be only Monday to try him.

Bright and clear rose the sun on the morning of the Fourth of July. Heavy and heroic boomed the one old cannon from Vineyard Hill. Merrily rang the bell of the village church, and, with its early peals, Max bounded over the fields, the shortest way to Quinny Ford's. Mrs. F. was at the well, drawing water.

"Yes, or no?" shouted he, as soon as he was within ear-shot. Mrs. Ford smiled so pleasantly and cheerfully, that he knew Quinny was to go before she answered, —

"Well, I think I shall run the risk, if you'll take good care of her."

"O, good!" cried Max, — "does she know?"

"No; I thought you ought to have the pleasure of telling her."

"O, good-er!" and he clapped his hands, and darted by Mrs. Ford, — but she caught him.

"Now, just look here, young man. Don't you go capering into the house like a wild Indian, and bounce upon her all of a sudden, and put her all in a flurry, you!"

"I'll be just as quiet as a kitten. See, now!" and he smoothed down his face with his hands and looked exceedingly sober.

Mrs. Ford laughed, and he walked away in a very dignified manner. But the little fellow was so happy that he stopped with his hand on the door-knob, and laughed to himself, all alone, as heartily as could be, for very joy, or, as he afterwards told his mother, "to get the laugh out of him," before Quinny should see him. When he did march into the room it was with a very demure face. Quinny was half sitting, half lying, on a kind of lounge, and looking rather sad.

"Hullo, Quinny!" said he, gayly.

"O, Max, I wish you a happy Fourth of July," said she, trying to be gay.

"My stars! don't I wish *you* one though! O, Quinny, we're going to have such a splendid time! Want me to tell you all about it?"

"O, yes! — I wish you would. You never have told me a word."

"Well, you see," said Max, blushing and feeling very warm and guilty, and twisting himself about in all sorts of ways, for fear his secret should be out before he was ready,— " you see, Quinny, I — I — well, I'll tell you now. We're going to the Ponds, and it's to be a children's pic-nic. There'll be big folks there, but we shall have our say; and there's bushels of candy, — and, O me! the plum-cake and frosted cake,— and one's got a great meeting-house on it, or something, — *that* came from Boston, — and nuts, and oranges, and all the girls are going to wear wreaths on their heads, and the boys have oak-leaves on their hats, — here's mine, — and O, there's oceans and barrels of lemonade, and we're going to play foot-ball and swing ———"

He stopped, fairly out of breath. Quinny's eyes danced sympathetic. "And, Quinny," continued he, coming nearer, and pretending to feel sorry, "you know I said I would stay at home with you; but you see I did not know we were going to have such times, and all the nice things, and I believe I must go."

Quinny tried to say that she wished him to go, but something came in her throat, and she could not speak. Something came into her wistful blue eyes, too, which Max saw, and he could bear it no longer, but roared out,—

"O, Quinn! — you're going, too!"

"W-h-a-t?" cried Quinny, in a tone almost as loud.

"You're going! — your mother said so! We're going to haul you in the truckle-cart! — I've got it! You don't know anything about it! — Oh! Oh! Oh!" — and Max rolled over and over on the floor in a very undignified and hilarious manner. I don't know how long he might have stayed there, if Mrs. Ford had not come in and made him rather ashamed of himself. You know he was a little boy.

In due time the truckle-cart and its four happy horses drove up to the house in grand style. Mrs. Ford brought Quinny out, and placed her on the little seat. She was so much better, that she did not have to lie down; and she did look so pretty in her loose white dress, with her long, fair hair, and a little straw bonnet on her head, and her cheeks flushed with heat and pleasure. Max placed the reins in her hand, and gave her a long willow rod for a whip, and told her to use it whenever they did not go fast enough; and so, after many injunctions from Mrs. Ford that she should not "step a foot on the ground to walk," they started. It was a long mile, up hill and down, to Pleasant Pond; but happy hearts make nimble feet, and before long they saw the sparkle of its waters.

"Now, you see," said Max, drawing the carriage

up to a pair of bars, and unharnessing himself to take them down, "Nobody knows you're coming but us; and so we're not going the way the rest do, but round through the lot, and we shall come out on the other side of the hill, and then we'll come on them all of a sudden."

So, more slowly, but no less merrily, ankle-deep in the yielding grass, they trudged on, talking in whispers, just as if the people up in the grove were not as busy as they could be with their own talking, and would not have heard a coach-and-six rattling over the stones. At the foot of the hill they stopped, left the carriage under an oak-tree, and two of the boys formed a "lady's chair" with their joined hands, to carry Quinny. But the path was so narrow and uneven, that they could not get on very well, and Quinny was rather alarmed and uneasy.

"Now, you stop a minute," said Max, "I'll tell you how to fix it. I can carry Quinny myself, as nice as a button."

"O, I'm afraid you're not strong enough!" cried she, "I'm afraid you'll drop me."

"No, I won't; why, I could carry two of you, just as easy as nothing." He felt very large, and bold, and strong, just then; so he gathered her up in his sturdy arms, and with a very red face, and very puffing cheeks, and a very stout heart, bore

her up the hill, and right into the midst of the party, and sat her down triumphantly on the grass.

"Quinny Ford's come!—Quinny Ford's come!" rang from one end of the grove to the other; for Quinny was a general favorite, and, moreover, they had all felt very sorry for her, because they thought she would have to stay at home; so the pleasure was all the greater for being unexpected.

I cannot tell you how every moment of that long, summer day was full to overflowing with delight,— how Quinny sat on her mossy seat, like a queen on her throne,— how the children gathered around her when tired of playing, and sometimes when they were not tired, and chattered to their hearts' content,— how all the fathers and mothers spoke to her so kindly, drawn by the sweet little face, that looked so happy, and grateful, and timid,— how the nicest cake, and candy, and oranges, were heaped upon her, twice as much as she could eat,— how she would quite have forgotten that she was lame, — only Max, vibrating like a pendulum between her and the players, never left her without saying, "Now, Quinny, you mind. Don't you stir a step!" and though she always answered, "No, I won't," and though when he came back he found her in the same place, it did not make a bit of difference. He seemed to think it was the only way he could fulfil his promise to her mother, — so he said every time just the same, "Now, Quinny, don't you stir!"

THANKSGIVING-DAY.

THE SPOILED DINNER.

"O I know something! I know something!" exclaimed little Meg Mayland, skipping into the sitting-room one morning.

"The dickens you do!" said Martial, throwing back his head in mock astonishment.

"Yes, I do, and you don't."

"My dear child," continued Martial, with an assumption of the gravest dignity, "it is quite preposterous to suppose that a person of your years and acknowledged character should be the receptacle of profound and important secrets; consequently, if you do know anything, it is your bounden duty to divulge. *Comprenez vous?*"

"I know something, and you don't," repeated Meg, utterly unable to understand the drift of Martial's remark, and wisely falling back on what was within the sphere of her comprehension.

"Meg," said Erne, looking up from her drawing, "Martial wants you to tell him what it is, that's all. Tell us, there's a dear."

"No, a'n't going to tell."

"You a'n't, eh? Look here, young woman — don't be in a hurry — hoity-toity — not quite so fast"; for Martial had caught the two little wrists, and twisted his feet round the two little legs, and Meg struggled manfully to get away.

"No, I sha'n't tell you. Mamma told me not."

"And how came she to confide in you, pray?"

"O, I was behind the window-curtain, and she did not know it, and — "

"Eaves-dropping!"

"No, I was n't dropping eaves either; but she came in, and I heard her tell Agnes; and she said, 'Don't tell the children, because if anything happens we sha'n't go'; and I came out, and there I was, and I asked mamma what it was, and she said, 'O, you little a'n't-good-for-anything! how came you here?' and I said I could n't help it, and she said, 'Well, then, I must n't tell *you*,' and I said no indeed I would n't, and then she told me perhaps we would all go to grandpapa's to spend Christmas, if Aunt Ellen is well enough; and you are not going to be told till just the day before, and I a'n't going to tell you either — O me! I *have* told! O me! what *will* mamma say to me?" and poor Meg stopped aghast, suddenly conscious that she had told the very secret over which she had been so loudly exulting.

Martial and Erne laughed, but it was no laughing matter with Meg.

"Do you think mamma will be very angry?" said she tremulously. "What do you suppose she will do?"

"O, nothing more than make you stay at home Christmas, when we go to grandpapa's, or something of that sort."

"O, pshaw! Martial," said Erne, "you sha'n't torment her so. It's no such thing, Meg, she —" But their mother came in at that moment, and Martial began to jump up and down, imitating Meg, and crying "O mamma! such a great secret; we're going to grandpapa's, Christmas, and none of us know anything about it but Meg." Meg looked on, anything but amused, with sorrowful tears in her brown eyes.

"I did n't mean to tell, mamma; I did n't know I told till — till I *had* told."

Her mother laughed. "Never mind, dear, now. You cannot untell it, so we will make the best of it."

"Mamma?"

"Well, dear?"

"I sha'n't have to stay at home when the rest go?" Meg was crying outright.

"Stay at home! No, indeed; what for, pray?"

"Martial said so, — perhaps."

"O, nonsense! Martial shall have his ears boxed, and you shall do it; there, run now and box them soundly. You did n't mean to disobey mamma, I know"; and Meg, overjoyed, jumped at Martial's ears, and he kept her off, and Erne ran to help her, and I don't know how it did turn out at last.

It was a merry gathering at the old home-farm on Christmas Eve. There were grandpapa and grandmamma, so glad to see them, and Uncle James and Aunt Matty, with their baby; and Aunt Carry, with her pale face and black dress, yet gentle and happy, and her only child, Jarvis, dressed very nicely; and there were Uncle Israel and Aunt Mary, with five sturdy boys; and Uncle Sinclair and his two children, Henrietta and Samuel; and Uncle Arthur with no child at all. Aunt Ellen was there, to be sure, but she lived there all the time, so I do not reckon her as company; but there was another person who did not live there all the time, and who was neither aunt, nor uncle, nor cousin to any one of them, but who still seemed to be very much interested in the family. He was called Mr. Ferguson. The children were rather bashful at first, and sat still, and at length went to bed very quietly; but the next day they made acquaintance rapidly.

"Aunt Ellen," said little Meg, as she sat on the arm of the sofa, combing her aunt's hair, "Is Mr. Ferguson my uncle?"

"No, dear," said she, laughing.

"He is n't my aunt, is he?"

"Not a bit —"

"Well, I don't see what he is here for, then."

"Why, don't you like him?"

"O yes, I like him; but we are uncles and aunts here, and he is n't."

"Are you my uncle and aunt?"

"O no, but *he is n't.*"

"All in good time," called out Mr. Ferguson, from the next room. Meg had not noticed that the door was open, and she was quite abashed at his merry laugh.

"I 'm going to kiss you," said he, coming towards her. Meg drew back.

"What! don't you like to kiss?" Meg shook her head.

"But I saw you kiss Aunt Ellen twice this morning."

"O," said Meg, "I kiss womans, but I don't kiss mans," and she jumped down and ran away.

When they came home from church, the next day, grandmamma called all the children round her and said: "Young people, I have a plan to propose. You know at the breakfast-table this morning we were very much crowded. How should you like to have a table set for you separately, in the kitchen?"

"Eat all alone, by ourselves?" said Erne.

"Yes, dear."

"But have turkey, and pudding, and cranberry-tart, just the same as the grown-up people?" said rosy-cheeked Joe.

"Yes, indeed, a whole turkey, all your own, and a pudding made expressly for you, and something else too."

"O, I should like it, I should like it!" they cried, all but Miss Henrietta Sinclair, who seemed extremely dissatisfied with the arrangement, — she thought herself, at fifteen, quite too old to be classed with children in that way.

"I am sure, grandmamma, the *children* might have a *side table*, and the rest of us all sit together. It will be so disagreeable to eat dinner with nobody to take care of so many boys."

"If you prefer to sit at my table, my dear, I am quite willing you should."

"I am sure I *do* prefer it."

"If Henrietta does, I will," said Samuel.

"If you please," said grandmamma, calmly. — Samuel blushed.

"But can't I?"

"Certainly, there will be room for you two, — does any other one wish to sit at my table?" But no one did, so they were dismissed.

"I wish you would eat with us," said Erne, "it is so much nicer."

Erne rather looked up to Henrietta, and addressed her with considerable deference.

"I don't think it is nicer," said Henrietta, tossing her head. "I am not used to living with children, and servants, and eating in the kitchen."

"I dare say grandmamma's kitchen is as good as your dining-room," exclaimed Cousin Gerry, who was indignant at Henrietta's sneer. Erne was shocked.

"You don't know anything about it," answered Henrietta. "You never were at our house in your life. We have an elegant carpet in our dining-room, and arm-chairs, and a sideboard, and everything, — and you say that it is no better than this country kitchen."

"Well, it is n't," said Gerry, sturdily, "nor half so good. I'd rather have grandpapa's sunshine than all your fine things. Mamma said your dining-room was as gloomy as a prison, and as cold as a barn."

"Gerry, you're crazy," was all the reply Henrietta deigned to make.

"And that is n't the worst of it," continued Samuel, "for if we drop a crumb, Laman makes such a fuss, you can't think."

"Who is Laman?" asked Ephraim.

"She's a horrid old scrag that takes care of us and worries us to death, only Hen. has grown up out of her reach a little, and she can't tyrannize over her so much, and so she makes up on me; but I play her a trick once in a while."

"But I shouldn't think you would want to sit at the grown-up table," said Martial. "Why don't you come with us?"

"Of course I shall; I only wanted to bother Hen., because she hates to have me tagging round after her."

"I'll just tell you how it is," said Henrietta, who considered Martial the only one whose age and attainments made his opinion of any value: "If I ever take Sam to a party, or ever a gentleman calls on me, Sam is sure to remember everything I say or do, and then make fun of it afterwards; so I tell papa it's more than it's worth to have him about."

Sam laughed heartily, but did not consider it worth while to deny the assertion. Their conversation was interrupted by the dinner-bell, and with a deal of bustle, and talking, and laughing, and hustling of chairs, they took their places.

"Who's going to sit at the head of the table?" called Martial.

"Erne Mayland, of course."

"No," said Aunt Mary, "Henrietta is the oldest, and she must have the seat of honor."

"She isn't coming," cried Gerry, "she is a young lady, — she can't eat in the kitchen."

"Gerry, Gerry," said his mother, reprovingly, but she went into the dining-room and found Henrietta.

"What is this dear?" said she, kindly, "don't you want to eat with the rest of the children?"

"Yes, of course she does," said her father, before Henrietta had time to speak.

"No, sir, I don't, I would rather eat with grandmamma."

"Nonsense, go along with the rest, my child."

"She thinks she's too old," cried Sam, from the door-way.

"Too old! bless the child!" murmured grandpapa, patting her neck.

Henrietta did not move till her father gave her a look, which was not to be misunderstood, and then, with tears of vexation in her eyes, she walked slowly out.

"Had to come, didn't you?" whispered Sam, provokingly.

"Stop," cried she, with rising anger, but Sam hummed quite audibly,—

> "Mamma, will you please to spread
> A little sugar on my bread?
> And mamma, dearest, if you please,
> To cut a little bit of cheese.
> I'm grown too old now to be carried;
> To-morrow, ma, may n't I be married?"

It was very exasperating in Sam, but it scarcely justified the stinging and very unlady-like blow, which made his ears tingle and burn for several minutes.

As soon as Henrietta came out, Erne left her seat at the head of the table to give it to Henrietta, and Martial left his at the foot and proceeded, with a very flourishing bow and great formality of manner, to conduct her to her seat, but Henrietta snatched her hand away, and would neither be conducted nor consoled.

"Do sit here," said Erne, timidly.

"I won't," was the sole reply, and she dropped into a vacant chair.

Martial stood still a moment, gave the lowest little bit of a prolonged whistle, and resumed his seat.

"Snubbed!" whispered Sam.

"Snubbed!" reiterated Martial.

Erne reluctantly took her place again, and Henrietta began to pout.

The turkey was contemplated with rapture. "It's our whole turkey," exclaimed Meg, clapping her chubby hands.

"Do sit still, and not poke your hands in my face," snapped Henrietta. Meg looked exceedingly sober for five minutes.

"I know where this cranberry-sauce came from, said Ephraim, don't you, Merrill?"

"Down in our meadows, eh?"

"Yes, don't you remember. O, Martial, you ought to have been there, — we got into a ditch and got wet and muddy up to our knees."

"Rather be here," said Martial, succinctly, helping himself to another spoonful of the sauce. "Better picking cranberries with a spoon from a bowl than with fingers from a ditch."

"They are luscious," said Sam, smacking his lips, "and they are splendid to color with."

"I know something else they are good for, too," said Ephraim, looking up from a turkey-wing.

"Tarts?" suggested Sam.

"Pies?" queried Martial.

"Worse than that," replied Ephraim.

"Worse!" cried Jerry. I don't call that bad, in the first place."

"I guess you'd call this bad, and worse, too, if you had 'em."

"What is it, then? Tell."

"Give it up?"

"Yes. Too much trouble to think when there's important business on hand."

"Corns!"

"Whew!" murmured Martial, only half suppressing a laugh.

"Fact," continued Ephraim, unconcernedly. "Ma had 'em and put 'em on, and they drew 'em out like a yoke of oxen."

"You vulgar boy! exclaimed Henrietta, attempting to look daggers at her cousin. It was the first remark she had made since she sat down. Poor Ephraim was quite unconscious of having said anything improper, and he blushed to the very roots of his hair.

"Go it Hen-pen!" sung out Sam, "nail your colors to the mast, and give it to 'em."

"O, Sam, please don't," begged Erne. "Never mind Ephraim. He didn't mean any harm, you know," she whispered to Henrietta.

"I don't care what he meant," muttered that amiable young lady, but loud enough to be heard around the whole table. "He's a brute, and not fit to be seen with decent people!"

"*Et tu brute!*" whispered Martial, but *not* loud enough to be heard, except by the two or three in his immediate vicinity, who, however, set up a private giggle, to the discomposure of Erne, who feared lest it should annoy Henrietta. The poor child was already beginning to find her honors rather burdensome.

"It isn't polite to whisper in company," said she, smilingly.

"It is n't fashionable to be polite here," answered Gerry.

"O, Meg, do sit still! you are spilling your dinner all over my dress," jerked Henrietta again. Meg looked deprecatingly at Erne.

"Maggy, dear, go sit by Martial, and let Frank take your place, he is so quiet."

"Yes, I will," said Meg, with great alacrity, and she jumped down from her high chair, plate in hand, spilling the mashed potatoes and sauce indiscriminately on the carpet and Henrietta's dress.

"Goodness me!" cried she, "what a mess! what a confusion! Erne, if you 're going to sit at the head of the table and govern a parcel of children, why can't you do it, and not have them running around like cats and dogs?"

"Better run round like cats and dogs than fight like them," retorted Martial. His flashing eyes met those of Henrietta, with no love in them. He was extremely fond of his sisters, though he loved to tease them a little, and Erne's painfully burning cheeks and downcast eyes roused his indignation to the damage of his reputation for politeness.

Little Meg edged in her chair by him and whispered confidentially, "I think cousin Henrietta is cross."

"I think cousin Henrietta is a bear," responded Martial, "a prowling, white Polar bear." This made Meg laugh.

"What are you laughing at?" said Samuel.

Meg looked half frightened at Martial.

"Only a little pleasant conversation between ourselves," replied he.

"I am glad there is anything pleasant at this table."

"I've asked John twice for the bread," spoke Henrietta again, "and now he has chosen to go into the dining-room and I haven't got it yet. I should think if we had to eat in the kitchen, we might have a servant to wait on us."

"O, I'll get it for you," cried Erne, delighted to please her cousin, and she jumped up at once and brought the bread.

"Why, what are you thinking of?" exclaimed Henrietta. "At the head of the table and passing the bread! Do you mean to be lady of the house and waiter too, or don't you have any servants at home?"

"I — John is gone —" faltered Erne. Henrietta helped herself to a generous slice of bread, and gradually ate herself into a better humor; but the cloud which had gathered over the merry company could not be dispersed. Sam tried to joke, and Gerry laughed, but Martial was angry, and Ephraim uncomfortable, and Erne entirely disheartened, and even Meg had been so "snubbed," as Sam would have said, that her prattling tongue was still. Henrietta would have talked and laughed, after she had thrown off her fit of ill-humor, for she was naturally gay and lively, but there was no response to her sallies.

The "something else" which grandmamma spoke of was a set of cranberry tarts, one for each child, on which he found the initials of his own name. This seemed to revive their drooping spirits, and they examined each other's tarts with considerable interest; but again poor little ill-starred Meg, in running round to Erne to show her " very own pie," caught her foot in Henrietta's dress and fell. She was not hurt in the least, and did not injure the dress, and as Henrietta was no longer sullen, she had no intention of scolding her, and did not speak a cross word; but Meg, judging from the past, expected a volley, and so she anticipated it by setting up a prodigious shriek and cry, which brought their elders from the dining-room, and broke up the dinner party in disorder.

Mrs. Mayland carried Meg to her own room and soothed her, and Martial and Erne soon followed.

Her mother noticed Erne's disturbed face, and inquired if anything had gone wrong.

"No, mamma — only — that is — " and Erne broke down and cried in right good earnest, which set Meg off again. Her mother began to be alarmed, but Martial told her it was "only that hateful Henrietta Sinclair, that spoiled everything," and he gave a detailed account of the affair. She palliated Henrietta's fault as much as possible, telling him how her mamma had died when Sam was a baby, and she had been left to the care of hired nurses, because her papa was unwilling to have her leave him, till Martial was mollified, and even pitied Henrietta, and Erne said she should never feel so unhappy about it again.

Children, you see it is quite possible for a turkey to be very well dressed, and puddings perfectly done, and pies just what they should be, and yet a little ill-humor may make of it all A Spoiled Dinner.

FOREFATHERS' DAY.

THE ARGUMENT.

"WHAT are all these pins stuck into the back of the sofa for?" lazily inquired Gerry Varse, as he lay swinging his legs over the arm of the sofa, kicking his heels against it, and in various ways illustrating the truth of the "divine Watts" — "For Satan," &c. (assuming that what is true of hands is equally true of heels.)

"Let them alone, sir!" thundered Martial, with more strength of lungs than his pale face seemed to indicate. He was just recovering from severe illness, and the color had not yet come back into his cheeks.

"You need n't cry before you 're hurt," answered Gerry. "A cat may look upon a king; and I don't suppose my looking at them will take off the heads of your pins."

"Your handling them will. You 're always pulling things to pieces. Get off the sofa, now, I want to come there."

"O, pshaw! Possession is nine points of the law."

"Is it? — well, there now!" and by a dexterous manœuvre, without any great exertion, Martial succeeded in landing Gerry on the carpet, and took the sofa himself. "You see," he remarked, with a metaphysical air, "possession may be nine points of the law, but so long as it is n't the tenth, your position is un-ten-able."

"O you coward!" said Gerry, good-humoredly, "you reckon on your weakness. You know I won't attack you, because you are sick; so you do anything. But I have a good long list of accounts scored up against you get well."

"Most likely you 'll get scoured yourself, when I get well; but see, here is a regular pitched battle. You know, Napoleon used to fight with pins, — so, why should n't I?"

At the word "battle," their little cousin Jarvis, from New York, who was visiting them, jumped up from the floor, and ran to see what was going on.

"Who is the pitched battle?" he asked eagerly.

"'Who?'— you little muff, look here; don't you see? Here it is,— the battle of the pins. These red-heads are the British,— I stuck 'em with sealing-wax; and the bright ones are the American officers; and the crooked ones, and the no-headed and brassy-looking things, and the black ones,— those are the rank and file of the American army, the bone and sinews of our land, sir; the bulwarks of liberty, sir, who will fight to the last drop of their blood, —

> 'Fight till the last armed foe expires,
> Fight for your altars and your fires,
> Fight for the green graves of your sires,
> God and your native land!' ——

"Sir!"

Jarvis gazed with saucer eyes, open mouth, and sympathetic, moving lips, and did not at all understand Gerry's merry laugh.

"Martial Mayland in a state of patriotism! Vive le Mayland!" and he tossed little Jarvis as high as avoirdupois would permit fourteen years to do.

"Tell me all about it," said Jarvis, when Gerry had subsided. "I do like to hear about wars and battles."

"Well, small boy, you know what day it is."

"Yes, it's Tuesday or Wednesday, I —"

"No, no; it's neither Tuesday nor Wednesday, nor any other day but Forefathers' Day, before which Tuesdays and Wednesdays, and all commonplace days 'pale their ineffectual fires,' eh?"

"Now you know all about it," interposed Gerry. "'No?' what a heathen! Then I must enlighten you. Come here, where nobody can hear us"; and in a loud whisper he began: "A great many years ago ——"

"Yes," whispered Jarvis, just as loud, "that's the way I like to have stories begin."

"Keep still, then, or that's the way my story will end. A great many years ago, as the crow flies, — it is a dreadful motto. It makes you feel all over. It has no more expression on me than a toad wants a tadpole, every bit and grain. Moral: Cabbages is not good for ginnipigs. Vide R. Bazalgette."

Jarvis's face was absolutely comical, in its intense wonder.

"Now, little cousin," said Martial, "he's making game of you. You know *me!* You know I am as true as steel, and never look one way and talk another. Just come here, young shuttlecock, and I'll tell you a true story which shall make your hair stand on end."

Jarvis went back rather ruefully, and took a cricket. "Now let it be real true," said he, "and about a battle."

"If there's to be fighting, I'm in for it," exclaimed Gerry, and he drew his rocking-chair so that he could put his feet on the sofa, and give Martial an occasional admonitory nudge. "All ready! — fire away, Historian of the Nineteenth Century."

"A great many years ago ——"

"O, that's the way Gerry's began," whined Jarvis.

"And did n't you say you liked it?" demanded Gerry, fiercely.

"Yes, — but — but — I don't want another just like it so soon."

"Hold still, and I'll branch off directly. A great many years ago, when there was nobody here but Indians —"

"Here, in this house?"

"No, there was no house here, and nothing but trees, and Indians, and wild bears, and catamounts, and such things. The king and folks in England got so bad that they could n't stand it."

"What did they do?"

"Just what I am going to tell you, if you'll hold your tongue long enough. They came over here."

"No; but I mean what did the king do that was so bad?"

"O, he oppressed the people, and imprisoned them, — and — and trained on like sixty. Enlarge a little on that point, Gerry."

"Why," continued Gerry, taking up the parable, "things had been running down hill generally, a good while. Hullo! we're having an audience," — for Erne and Meg had come in to play, but growing interested, came and "squatted" on the floor, instead. "Well, I trust I shall be found adequate to the emergency. Well, as I said, things had been running down hill a good while. The king and his party wanted to get all the power on their side, and the people wanted to get the power on their side, and so they went at it, shovel and tongs."

"They did n't fight with shovel and tongs?" said Jarvis, incredulously.

"Figuratively," nodded Gerry.

"How is that?" persisted Jarvis.

"Not at all," answered Erne.

"Did n't they fight at all?" turning to Martial, as a last resort.

"Fight? Yes, fought like mad!" rejoined Gerry.

"Now, Martial, I wish you would do the telling," said Erne, "and Gerry, keep still; I can't make out one thing or another, by him, — that is, I can, but Jarvis can't, nor Meg. They can't take him as I can."

"Well, I will; keep still, Gerry, now. You see there had been a struggle a long while. It was n't all of a sudden. It had come down from the middle ages, and the end ages too, for aught I know, only it came to a head then."

"When?"

"Why, in the time of Charles the First, or along there. That was two hundred years ago, more or less, — it does n't matter much, any way. You see, the king kept pulling his way, and the people their way, till finally all the good ones said they would n't stand it any longer, and they came off to America."

"O, what a whopper!" sighed Gerry.

"Hullo! what's the matter now?"

"All the good people came to America!"

"Well, did n't they? — all the best?"

"No, indeed, they did n't. Just as good people stayed behind as those that came over. I tell you what it is, *I* think there's a great deal more fuss made about our forefathers than they deserve."

"O Gerry!" exclaimed Erne, shocked.

"Yes, I do. Hang me, and draw me, and quarter me, if you like; I'll stick to it. Why, just see, now, which deserves the most credit, a man who takes his money and runs when he sees his house on fire, or a man who stays and tries to get his father and mother safe, and put out the fire, and not get the house burnt, or, at any rate, save the barn?"

"Well, but suppose you can't put the fire out, and the more you try to do it the more other people blow it, and put the wood on, — what then?"

"Then you ought to work all the harder."

"I say, if you were in a country, and a strong party was against you, and you could n't do what was right, and had to be no better than a slave, I say, if you can get off anywhere where you can have your own way, you ought to go."

"And I say that it's right down selfish in anybody to clear out and just look after themselves, and let all the rest stay behind and take it."

"But could n't the rest have gone too, if they had chosen, I should like to know?"

"But that is n't the way to benefit your country. The wickeder she is, the more you ought to stay and help her through."

"Lot did n't, any way."

"Hang Lot!"

"Why, Gerry!" exclaimed Erne, "are n't you ashamed? You sha'n't talk so, — I'll tell mother."

"He's run aground, you see," laughed Martial. "He can't say anything else, so he says that."

"I'm not run aground, either; but you go bringing up Lot; and what's he, or any of those fellows, that lived nobody knows when, to do with it? The case is entirely different. He had an angel sent straight to him expressly, and we have to go by our own judgment."

"Well, you'll confess this, that if our forefathers had n't come over, we should n't have had this nation."

"No, I don't confess any such thing. If they had stayed at home, and helped steer the ship through the breakers, she might have come out fair and square, and England have been a great deal freer and better off than she is now; though, to be sure, she is well enough off now. And then, when she began to be overfull, people might have come over here in peace, and founded this nation, and never had any Revolution."

"I don't believe a word of it," said Martial.

"Neither do I," said Erne — "I have read history, and it always says that our forefathers were noble, and heroes, to come over here in the cold winter, and leave home and everything to found a nation that could be free, and leave it to their children; and I don't believe you know more than the histories."

"You little goose! I don't say I do, and I don't say they were n't noble, and heroes; but I say they would have been nobler, and greater heroes, if they had stayed at home, and fought it out there, and made their own country free, and helped their countrymen, instead of running away, and setting up for themselves, and leaving the rest in the lurch."

"I don't believe it," persisted Erne.

"You need n't believe it," replied Gerry, a little nettled, — "I did n't say you were to believe it."

"If they had run away at the first blow," said Martial, "it would have been different; but they stayed as long as they thought there was any good in staying, and then they came off, and none too soon. They thought the truth, and freedom, and all that, was going to die, and they determined to bring it here, and keep it alive, if they could."

"You see it did n't die in England, though, even after they left it."

"Did they come all alone?" asked little Jarvis, to whom the long discussion was rather uninteresting.

"All alone? Why, they came all together, in a ship."

"I should think they would have been afraid, — only four of 'em."

"Four? Who said there were four?"

"You said so. You said four of our fathers came over in a ship."

"Four of our fathers! O me! — four of our fathers!" and all the children set up a shout that quite disconcerted Jarvis.

"You did say so!" said he, stoutly, — "you said four of our fathers fought like mad."

There was another burst of laughter, but Erne came to the rescue. "Forefathers, — f-o-r-e-fathers, not f-o-u-r. It means that they came over first, before anybody else, I suppose. But, dear me! there were more than four! — there were a hundred, were n't there, came over first? — a hundred and one in the Mayflower, — that was the name of the vessel. Come, now, we won't laugh at you again, Jarvis. Go on with your story, Erne."

"Where was I?"

"Somewhere about their coming over."

"O, yes! Well, they came over, any way, right or wrong, — right, *I* think, and had a horrid time, what with the captain, and the vessel, and the storm, and the ——"

"What was it all?" interrupted Jarvis.

"Why, the captain would n't take them where they wanted to go, and the vessel sprung a leak, and they had to go back, and O me! there was no end of trouble."

"Shows they 'd no business to come," muttered Gerry.

"But they succeeded splendidly, after all; so that shows they *had* business to come. And they got here the twenty-second of December, and it was cold as a barn, and nobody expecting them, and nothing ready, nor anything, and they had a right hard time of it, and that 's Forefathers' Day."

"What is Forefathers' Day?" queried Erne, mischievously, — "the hard time they had?"

"Don't you set up to joke!" and Martial shook his fist at her.

"That is n't all?" said Jarvis.

"That 's all of any account," answered Martial.

"I don't call that any story at all," pouted the disappointed little fellow.

"You ungrateful young rascal!"

"Why, there is n't any battle; and where 's all those pins?"

"O, that did n't come till afterwards. I can't tell you about that now, I 'm tired."

"I don't care anything about old Forefathers' Day," muttered Jarvis, who was in an ill-humor.

"Of course you don't," said Gerry; "you don't know anything about it. Never dealt in the article. Don't know what the feeling is. Never had a forefather. You 're nothing but a sauer-kraut Dutchman."

"I aint a Dutchman, either."

"Yes, you are a Dutchman, without any forefathers. None but New-Englanders have forefathers: so they 're hopping mad when we talk about ours. Poor little fellow! Come, now, I 'll tell you what I 'll do. You want a battle; so I 'll give you a real one, — a pitched battle with snowballs. I 'll lead the anti-Puritans. I think they ought to have stayed at home; Martial thinks they ought to have come. All on my side, come over here. All on his side, go to him."

"I 'm on his side," said Erne.

"So am I," said Meg, who always did what Erne did.

"So am I," chimed in Jarvis, who chose to be on the strongest side.

"Right is in the minority, as usual," said Gerry. "Now, Martial, you can't go out; so you must watch at the window, and let Erne be Vice-General, and I'll beat her and her forces single-handed, and we'll soon see whether four of our fathers would n't better have stayed at home."

But I think it would have been very difficult to decide that question by the winning side, for all four of them were soon down in the snow, rolling over and over, cramming the snow down each other's necks, in all sorts of fair and unfair ways, laughing, shouting, and screaming, to their hearts' content.

CHRISTMAS.

THE MAYLAND CELEBRATION.

"I DON'T care if you have got up to the head. You'd better have stayed where you were, for then the great patch on your elbow would not show, and now everybody has a good square look at it!"

Cruel, cruel words! and Robert Mayland's flushing cheek and trembling lips told how sharply they struck home. Thoughtless Stephen Osborne! He was angry with himself for having lost his place at the head of the class, and angry with Robert for gaining it, — too angry to be anything but glad at seeing he had made Robert unhappy, and he went on: "I guess I would stay at home before I would wear a jacket that had two different colors. Ho! ho! that's the way they do at the county-house!"

"I'd rather wear a jacket all the colors of the rainbow than be a dunce," retorted Robert; "and I'm going to have a new jacket at Christmas, too."

"Yes, and go without a turkey to pay for it. You can't afford it any other way. It will be your

Christmas present, I suppose; so you will kill two birds with one stone."

"It won't, either," rejoined Robert, though rather faintly, for there was some truth in Stephen's words.

"You did n't have any Christmas last year, and you are n't any richer now, I 'll be bound. I would n't give that (snapping his fingers) for all that you 'll find in your stocking."

Robert Mayland walked home alone and heavy-hearted. He was not old enough and wise enough to feel that Stephen's attempted ridicule was far more disgraceful to Stephen than to himself. The patch on his jacket looked larger and uglier than ever, and he forgot the gentle, noble, patient, widowed mother, who, in sorrow and loneliness, wrought on and toiled on for her five children. He only wished he were rich, and could have presents like the other boys; and as he sat toasting his feet before the fire that night, he saw wonderful pictures in the glowing coals, — as many and many a boy, ay, and many a man too, has done before him.

"What is it, Robert?" asked his mother, cheerily.

"Ma'am?"

"You were looking very thoughtful. What is it about?"

"O, mamma, I was only thinking."

"Of course you were," spoke up Martial. "No one would suppose you were doing anything else, staring there into the blaze with eyes as big as pewter platters. Let's know what is brewing."

"Not unless you choose, Robert," added his mother, quietly.

"O, I don't care, mother. It was only about — I was thinking — that is, I was wishing — we could have a merry Christmas once more."

"Just such nice ones as we used to have before dear papa went away, — so do I," said Erne, without looking up from the slate on which she was drawing. Neither she nor Robert saw the paleness that came across their mother's face; but Martial did, for he was older, and his mother's stay, and comfort, and companion. "I am sure we are very happy all the time," said he; "just as happy as we can be without papa."

"Only mamma has to work so hard," said Erne, mournfully.

"And we have to wear old clothes," added Robert, more mournfully.

"And don't have any nice Christmas," chimed in little Meg, most mournfully.

Mamma did not like to see the clouds hovering over her children's faces, so she quickly dispelled the one that had gathered on her own, and said cheerfully, "Whether we have nice Christmases or not, we will have a nice, warm supper to-night; so draw out the coals, Rob, while I get the potatoes."

Martial followed his mother into the pantry, shut the door after him and held the latch down. "Mamma," said he, earnestly, "I think it would be a good plan to have a Christmas." His mother looked at him, a little surprised. "I don't mind it for myself," he went on, "indeed I don't; but the children would enjoy it so much, and particularly poor little Agnes. Only think how much she is shut up, and does not see anybody scarcely but us, and does not have any pleasures." "Yet she is very happy," interposed her mother. "Yes, ma'am, I know it; but she would enjoy a Christmas so much, because it is all in the house, and she could be in the midst of it, just as much as if she were n't lame. And then, mamma, you think papa is happy in heaven, and don't you believe he would like to have us just as happy as we can be made?"

"Certainly, my dear; and I do not know but that I have done wrong in not making your lives livelier and merrier."

"O dear, no, mamma, we don't any of us want to be dancing a jig all the time. Only when every one else is hopping, why, Rob and Erne and Meg would like to join in, I suppose."

"Very natural, I know; and I think you are quite right about the Christmas. We will talk it over again at supper, but I must attend to preparing that now."

When they were all seated at the table, mamma said, "Well, little ones, Martial thinks we would better have a Christmas. What do you think of it?"

A great "O-o-oh!" was sounded in concert, and Erne jumped up, ran round to Martial, and, pulling his head over the back of his chair, began to kiss him.

"Out of the way! take yourself off!" he shouted; but instead of Erne's taking herself off, Meg jumped on, so that the poor fellow had to drag himself sidewise out of his chair, in order to be rid of them. When they were all quiet again, mamma went on, — "Now, children, you must decide what we shall do."

"O, I know," cried Robert; "have a big roast turkey and bushels of dressing, and a plum pudding, and cranberry tarts, and —"

"And eat your Christmas all up, like a glutton. Are n't you ashamed of yourself?" interrupted Erne. "Now, I say let the dinner go. You can't buy everything else, and a dinner too. Let's have —"

"Let's have a dinner, any way," said Robert,

"for Stephen Osborne said we could not afford a turkey, and I want to show him we can."

"And show yourself a goose at the same time, for we can't," added Martial.

"No, we'll have you roasted, and have a turkey and a goose too," and Erne smacked her lips.

"Softly, softly," said mamma. "I hope, Robert, we are not going to have a Christmas for the sake of showing that we are not poor." Robert blushed, for that was in fact the very reason, the main reason, why he wanted one.

"Because, in the first place," said Martial, "we are poor, and in the second place we are not ashamed of it, and in the third place it is none of Stephen Osborne's business whether we are or not."

"And if we only had dear papa with us," added Erne, "we should not care if we never saw a turkey or a chicken for a thousand years, nor any goose, either, except you, old Bobus," and she "chucked" him under the chin. He saw that the current was setting against the turkey; but the sturdy, sensible good humor of his brother and sister infected him, and he was stronger against Stephen Osborne than he had been when single-handed.

"Now, Erne," said Martial, "let's have your views on the subject."

"My views comprise, first, going to church in the morning, of course; a luncheon at noon, at which we will have soda biscuit, and nobody shall eat more than two, except Rob, who shall take an extra half to console him for the turkey; secondly, or thirdly, which is it? well, wherever it comes, a grand coasting-party in the afternoon, — we'll put Agnes into a feather-bed of blankets, and —"

"Perhaps there won't be any snow," suggested Robert.

"Of course there will; what would Christmas be worth without snow? Then in the evening we will have the grand — grand —"

"Splurge!" said Martial. "Gun!" whispered Robert.

"O, you dreadful boys! yes. We'll have apples, — we have plenty of them, — and all the nuts, roasted and fried, and we'll give presents —"

"Who?" asked Meg's rosy lips and eager eyes.

"Who? Why, everybody, of course; that is, except myself. Nobody need expect to get anything from me; but I hope you will all be generous towards me, considering my efforts as the oldest daughter."

"I'll spend my three-cent piece," said Meg; "that will buy three sticks of candy."

"And we'll each have a half, won't we?" laughed Martial.

"Now, Mr. Martial," said mamma, "we are ready to receive your proposition. The subject is still open for discussion."

"Ladies and gentlemen!" began Martial, rising and flourishing the half of a hot "lady-finger."

"I suppose I am the 'gentlemen,'" said Rob, in an under tone.

"I think he means himself," said Erne. "He is talking for his own benefit, not ours."

Martial waved his potato in a dignified manner, and went on. "I rise on this important occasion, to offer an amendment. (Here he stopped for a mouthful of potato, which, being disposed of, he proceeded.) The plan brought forward by the distinguished lady on my left, (a very low bow to Erne, which she acknowledged with a profound courtesy,) is no doubt very fine, but (another mouthful of potato) it lacks that brilliancy which I am happy to say is the distinguishing characteristic of the sterner sex. The plan which I am about to propose" (another mouthful) ——

"As soon as I have swallowed a bushel of potatoes," said Erne, mimicking his pompous tones.

"Small children, who cannot be quiet, are requested to be removed by their mothers. The plan which I am about to propose has for its chief feature, — its centre-piece, — a — a — I beg that I may not again be subjected to the ordeal of kisses, however much the female portion of my audience may approve ——"

"No danger," said Erne, "we can't get at your mouth, it's so running over with lady-fingers."

"Go ahead! shouted Robert, "I'll stand guard!"

"Ladies and gentlemen, I have the honor to suggest a — Christmas-tree."

"Splendid!" — "The very thing!" — "O yes, mamma, let's!" — came from all sides, and for a minute mamma could scarcely get in a word. "But, dear children," she said at length, "Christmas-trees don't grow all ready ——"

"Plenty in Burr woods," said Martial.

"With lights, and flowers, and presents all on, I suppose."

"O no! but you know, mamma, Rob and I can get the tree, a fine one, — it's a great deal to have a fine tree, and that won't cost anything; then we can get plenty of pitch-pine to burn on it, and that wont cost anything. Then the girls and we too, need not get any more presents than we were going to get in the first place, only what we do make we will put on the tree; and I should think four women might put their heads together and fit it up very pretty, without expending a fortune."

"And Agnes could help us a sight on that, could n't you, Aggy dear?" cried Erne.

"O yes, I can make ever so many things, while you are gone to school, — dolls and bags ——"

"O, you must n't tell, child. Everything must be kept the most profound secret. Nobody is to suppose he is going to have anything, and then we shall not be disappointed if we don't get anything."

"I shall," whined little Meg; "I shall be disappointed. I won't spend my three cents till I know."

"O you little Yankee," cried Martial; "hand over your three cents here. I'll be responsible for your receiving a present."

"And we could have the room dressed up with evergreen," said Robert.

"And I can make tissue flowers, and so can Agnes," added Erne.

"A tree or not a tree, that is the question," and Martial leaned back in his chair in a very grand way.

"A tree then be it, since you have set your hearts upon it," answered mamma. And then there was such leaping, and dancing, and clapping of hands, — such planning, and laughing, and wondering, till Meg was sent to bed by main force an hour after her usual time; and even the pale cheek of little Agnes was flushed with excitement.

The days rolled on, and our young people were busy as bees. Those who went to school hurried home the moment school was out, and gave themselves the shortest possible time for returning. Mrs. Mayland's silk-bag was turned inside out twenty times a day. Martial ransacked the garret, and upset everything. There were mysterious errands to the village "cheap cash store," — ends of paper packages peeping out from under shawls, — a general hiding and looking very anxiously and elaborately careless whenever a door was suddenly opened.

"Here's Aggy, mamma," said Erne one day, "has the advantage of all the rest of us, — I think it's too bad! She just sits at home safely and sews while we are at school, and we have to do our sewing by fits and starts."

"Agnes sew!" answered her mother, with pretended surprise. "I am sure Agnes seems to me to be cutting tissue flowers a great part of the time."

"O, now," exclaimed Robert, "you need not pretend, mamma. Aggy does not cut paper roses all the time, I know. Where did that skein of silk come from, I should like to know, that I picked up under her chair?"

"Aggy," said Martial, "tell me what you are going to give me, there's a dear!" and he sat down on the rug and took her feet in his hands.

"Lean forward then, and let me whisper," answered Aggy.

"No, no, don't tell, — you will lose all the fun!" cried Erne.

"O fie! just let Aggy and me alone, — now then! We are intimate friends, Aggy and I. Now then, come, — why don't you tell?" So Agnes put her mouth down to his ear, and said in a slow, distinct whisper, —

"I — am — going — to — give — you — a — little — *red box!*" and a pretty smart one it was, too. They all set up a laugh, — all but Martial, who put both hands up to his ears, and groaned, and made wry faces, as if he was very much hurt.

"I'm glad of it, O, I'm glad of it," cried Meg, delighted.

"Glad! what are you glad for, you young monkey?"

"Because you got cheated, and you're such a great boy," and Meg clapped her hands with joy. Martial growled, and crawled on all fours to the place where she was standing, and "tickled" her, and pinched her, (not very hard,) and tried to make her tell what she was going to give, but she would not. "But I *know* what I am going to give," said she, "and I know what Erne is going to give, because I sleep with Erne, and she has to tell me, because I see the things on the table, and Agnes's is the prettiest of all, and ——"

"Now stop, you gypsy, you," interrupted Erne, "you'll have it all out the next minute. Don't you presume to lisp a syllable, one way or the other. If you do!" and Erne shook her finger warningly. Meg shut her lips close, and pounded them together with her hand, to show how impossible it was for any words to come out.

"Well," said Martial, crawling back to the fire, "I see how it is. I am the worst abused fellow in this house. Nobody confides anything to me. I hope, however, nobody expects to get anything from me."

"Ho! I think we do," cried Agnes. "I wonder what is all that hammering in the wood-house for? — and what has become of all mamma's twine?"

"Yes, and where is my paint-box, I should like to know?" said Erne. "I have not set my eyes on it for two days, and mamma looks knowing, and won't tell."

"And I found a piece of pasteboard in the wood-room this morning," said Meg, "cut into all funny corners, and some paint on it."

"Nonsense, children, nonsense," said Martial. "Get your Arithmetic, Bob. I really cannot fritter away my time in this frivolous conversation."

And still the days rolled on, till it was only three days to Christmas, and the schools closed. And the red sun came up over the snowy hills, and it was only two days to Christmas, and up, slowly up again, and it was only one day to Christmas. Only one day to Christmas! and the tree was to be brought up, and the evergreens cut, — those were the first things. Erne would go down in the woods to help and see, — and they crashed through the crusted snow, and brought down snow-storms from the branches, and hesitated, and chattered, and decided, and hesitated, and decided again, and loaded the sled with evergreen, and carried the tree in their hands, — it was not a very large one, — and then it was to be trimmed, and hung, and prepared for lighting, and such a trouble to get the gifts on without the names being seen, — and they finally did not hang half, but gave them to mamma to put on the next day, when they were gone to church.

And once more the red sun rose joyous over the snowy hills, and it was Christmas, — the great feast-day of the world. Happy hearts, sparkling eyes, rosy cheeks, and nimble feet, went from Mrs. Mayland's cottage over the snowy hills, when the little children went to worship God in the village church. Full, clear, and wondrous sweet their young voices rang out with the organ peal. Mrs.

Mayland watched them from her window till even little Meg's blue cloak was out of sight, and then with a blessing on her lips and in her heart, she went back to pale little Agnes. But Agnes was sitting in the sunshine playing with her kitten, — sunshine beaming in through the window, sunshine beaming out through her eyes; so Mrs. Mayland, with a word and a caress, left her, and went on with the preparation of a wonderful pudding, whose existence was a secret to all but Agnes. There were many other things to be done also, but when the house had been put in order, and the Christmas-tree had received the last touch, and the neat little room was all ready to be lighted, and the door was locked, there yet remained two hours before the children would be at home. They had carried the soda biscuits with them, together with a few for a poor old lady who lived alone, and in whose house they were to take their lunch, and spend an hour or so to make her Christmas more merry, and then they were to take Meard Pond on their way home, where was some "tall sliding," Robert said. This arrangement had been proposed by Mrs. Mayland, partly for the old lady's happiness, partly for the children's, and partly to make the interval between their coming home and candle-light as short as possible, — as candle-light was to be the signal for the commencement of festivities.

Mrs. Mayland gave Agnes her bread and milk, and a book of pictures, and then went to her own room. She was very sad, and she wished to be alone. With her children's happy voices around her she was cheerful, but in the silence, she remembered a manly voice, that her heart was faint to hear again. Her thoughts travelled back to the Christmas three years before, when her children and their father gathered about the home-hearth. Then came the sad parting, — the far wandering over the sea, — the long waiting without tidings, — and last, the terrible tidings, — " wrecked," — " lost." Tears, often kept back for her children's sake, would now no longer be repressed, — she wept, and trembled, and shuddered, in the greatness of her sorrow. A knocking at the door aroused her. She hastily rose, calmed herself with a sudden and strong effort, and went to open the door to whatever neighbor had called. It was not a neighbor.

Over the snowy hills, flushed with the setting sun, came the eager children, rolling in the snow, stamping, snowballing, pushing each other down,— overflowing with vigorous young life, — and their presence soon filled the house. Their mother met them at the door, and kissed and embraced them with more than her usual tenderness. There was a glow on her face, and an almost startling brilliancy in her blue eyes.

"Mamma, how happy you look," said Erne.

"And how handsome!" added Martial.

"You are really glorified," continued Erne,—"something has happened."

"Yes, something has happened,— Christmas has happened. My darlings have come home again all safe. Shall I not be happy?"

"Why, yes, but it is not so very remarkable. You did not expect we were going to get lost or be torn in pieces by wild beasts coming home from church."

"Where's Aggy?" asked Martial, not seeing her in her accustomed place.

"She is in my room," said mamma; "she will be out directly. Come, dear children, take off your clothes,— it is almost dark."

"Why, mamma," said Erne, astonished, "Aggy in your room, in the cold?"

"Not in the cold, dear; I have had a fire kindled."

"In your room? O, that's nice; let's go in."

"No, no," said mamma quickly; "you must not go in. The truth is, a Christmas present has come while you were gone, and Aggy is in there looking at it."

"O, what is it, mamma?— do tell,— don't

wait," exclaimed Robert. "A Christmas present so valuable that it has to have a fire made for it!" puzzled Robert, — "it must be something alive. At least tell us where it came from. Did you order it, or who sent it?"

"God sent it, my child. The Christ whose birth we celebrate to-day." The tone was so solemn that the children were awed. Then their mamma smiled, but her eyes were full of tears, — yet happy tears, and she left the room.

"Well, I declare!" said Martial; "what does it all mean?"

"I never saw mamma act so in my life," said Erne. "A Christmas present! What can it be?"

"Nothing very bad, I think, for she is evidently happy; but I did not know a present of any kind could give her such a splendid color."

They stood by the fire talking, and Mrs. Mayland came in and out of the room, lighted the candles, stirred the fire, and the children saw that there was always a smile in her eyes. Presently she said, gayly, " Now, fellow-citizens, form a line. The exhibition is ready."

There was a good deal of laughing, and jolting, and jumping up and down, in eagerness to see the Christmas-tree first.

"Is it all lighted, mamma?" cried Meg.

"All lighted, my love."

"O, I wonder what I shall have. I know what you are going to have, and mamma,—a beautiful——"

"Hold your tongue," said Rob, shaking his fist menacingly.

They reached the door. Mrs. Mayland's hand was on the latch,—she hesitated.

"How you tremble, mamma," said Martial. "What *is* the matter?—you must be ill."

"Nothing, dear," answered she nervously. "Open the door. Go in,—quick!"

He opened the door. The light burst full upon them. They uttered an exclamation of delight, which suddenly, on Meg's lips, turned to a cry of terror, and she clung to her mother. The older children looked in the direction of her frightened glance, and there, close to them, a little in the shadow of the door, stood a tall, bearded man,—but not a robber, as Meg thought; O no, for little Agnes lay in his arms. One more glance up from the full beard and the bronzed cheeks into the dark eyes, and there was a cry and a rush,—"Papa!"

"And so you are our Christmas present?" said Erne, an hour after, when the first great gush of happiness and rapture and excitement and tears was over, and they all sat "in a heap," (as Martial said, but Erne had replied: "No matter,

is it, papa? You know we all want to touch you.")

"And that was what made mamma so handsome?"

"And how *did* you come, papa? Don't tell us all about everything. We will have that all along. O, the long winter evenings, — the blessed evenings we shall have all together, and you will talk to us, — but, tell us, papa, where you were when we came in, — and how you could keep still so long."

And he told them how he came to the cottage, and found mamma alone, — he did not tell them, because he could not, of that meeting; but he told how little Agnes was brought in, — little Agnes, his white lamb, whose great, calm, happy eyes were looking up into his then, like stars, — and how at first she did not know him, but soon came to him and nestled in his bosom, till her young, pure heart, beat close against his, — and then how mamma told him all about the children, and showed him their rooms, and their clothes, and their books and playthings, and the Christmas-tree, and how they came to have it, and then he heard their voices coming, and went into the parlor, and waited, and waited, pressing little Agnes closer and closer, till the door opened, and ——

Then he told them just a little of his long journeying, — the shipwreck — the almost miraculous manner in which he had been saved — the hardships he had endured — the long illness — the many perils, and the safe return, — all the particulars, as Erne said, he deferred to the " blessed winter evenings" that lay golden and shining before them.

" And now, little ones, you have forgotten the Christmas-tree ; but shall we not examine it ? "

" O yes, papa," said Erne, " but we will have another Christmas-tree at New Year, just for you."

" And we shall have to hang ourselves on it," said Martial, " for we have hung all our property on this one."

They walked round the room, admiring it, and it really looked very pretty, with its evergreen festoons and roses, — and then there was a demand on Meg's part for the gifts. Martial took charge of their distribution. " Miss Margaret Mayland's " name was read, and she was called up so often, that no doubt existed in her own, or any one else's mind that she had received ample remuneration for the disbursement of her three cents. Martial's hammering was accounted for by the appearance of a curious little affair, — half truckle-cart, half sled ; or rather, all truckle-cart one half the time, and all sled the other ; on one side of which was painted in bright green letters, " Agnes Mayland," and on the other, " The Arrow." This was made so that

Agnes could be cushioned and blanketed in to any extent. There was a painted pasteboard horse for Meg, and a varnished work-box for Erne, and a kite for Robert, all made by Martial, the latter "rather out of season," he said, " but it was well to have an anchor to the windward." There were also needle-books, and pincushions, and pasteboard baskets covered with silk, and a spool-box for mamma, and many, many things, invented by active brains, and wrought by loving hands, which cost very little money, but were just as precious, for all that.

Nine, ten, eleven o'clock came, and nobody wished to go to bed, and neither papa nor mamma could bear to send the children away; but Agnes and Margaret were both asleep, and so mamma said they must all go. Before they went, they knelt and poured out their full hearts in praise and thanksgiving to Him who had gathered them once more, — an unbroken family. So their Christmas ended. Nay, rather, so their Christmas burst into the bloom of a thrice happy New Year.

And so, little children everywhere, may merry Christmases bud and blossom for you into happy and ever happier New Years.

Cambridge: Stereotyped and Printed by Welch, Bigelow, & Co.

www.ingramcontent.com/pod-product-compliance
Lightning Source LLC
Chambersburg PA
CBHW030311170426
43202CB00009B/958